Marked for God's Commanded Blessing!

I Am A Child Of God

Published by
Morris Cerullo World Evangelism
Copyright© 2000
San Diego, California
Printed in the United States of America

Morris Cerullo World Evangelism
P.O. Box 85277
San Diego, CA 92186-5277

Morris Cerullo World Evangelism
P.O. Box 3600
Concord, Ontario L4K 1B6

Morris Cerullo World Evangelism
P.O. Box 277, Hemel Hempstead
HERTS • HP2 7DH

Dedication

Dedicated to my faithful partners who have sown precious seed into the worldwide outreaches of Morris Cerullo World Evangelism. May you receive God's Hundred-fold return.

TABLE OF CONTENTS

PERSONAL

My dear Precious Partner,

Every so often - The Heavens
open - and our Lord, thru
the power of The Holy Spirit,
give's A mighty Revelation,
that is Destined to change
The Lives of His People.

This Revelation - "You are Marked
for God Blessing" - is Just that.

It is my God Calling - to Share
This Message with you —
      Knowing - when you open
Your heart, Receive the Message
Then Act on the Message -
Your Life, Your Family, Your Ministry
Will Never Be The Same —
                    Your Partner for Souls
      God Bless You Morris.

Believe in The Lord Your God - So Shall
Ye Be Established, Believe His prophets
So Shall Ye Prosper! II Chron. 20/20

INTRODUCTION

*"To every thing there is a season, and a time to every purpose
under the heaven: a time to be born, and a time to die; a time to
plant, and a time to pluck up that which is planted."*
Ecclesiastes 3:1-2

THIS IS YOUR SEASON!

Throughout the ages there have been seasons when God has
fulfilled specific purposes within the lives of His chosen people.

When Moses and the children of Israel were wandering through
the wilderness, it was a season of testing and preparation for the
time they would enter the Promised Land and take possession of
their inheritance.

During that season, God revealed Himself as the God of
supernatural provision. He fed them daily with heavenly manna.
He led them by a pillar of cloud by day and a pillar of fire at night.

When they needed water, He caused water to gush out of a rock.
He supernaturally provided for all their needs. Their clothes did
not wear out, nor did their feet swell. (Deuteronomy 8:4)

God determined a set time of forty years: one year for each day they searched for land. God said, *"And your children shall wander in the wilderness forty years, and bear your whoredoms, until your carcasses be wasted in the wilderness. After the number of the days in which ye searched the land, even forty days, each day for a year, shall ye bear your iniquities, even forty years, and ye shall know my breach of promise." Numbers 14:33-34*

Because of their disobedience they wandered in the wilderness forty years and an entire generation died and were unable to enter the Promised land.

During that season of forty years in the wilderness, God fulfilled specific purposes in the lives of the children of Israel. He tested them to see what was in their hearts and whether or not they would be obedient to Him.

As they prepared to enter the Promised land, Moses told them, *"And thou shalt remember all the way which the Lord thy God led thee these forty years in the wilderness, to humble thee, and to prove thee, to know what was in thine heart, whether thou wouldest keep his commandments, or no." "And he humbled thee, and suffered thee to hunger, and fed thee with manna, which thou knewest not, neither did thy fathers know; that he might make thee know that man doth not live by bread only, but by every word that proceedeth out of the mouth of the LORD doth man live. Deuteronomy 8:2-3*

When the forty years was over, God spoke to them, *"...Ye have dwelt long enough in this mount: Turn you, And take your journey,..." Deuteronomy 1:6-7*

He told them, *"Behold, I have set the land before you; go in and possess the land." Deuteronomy 1:8*

Joshua led a new generation into a new season. The children of Israel entered into a season whereby they were conquering their enemies and taking possession of the Promised Land.

They entered a new season of taking possession of God's promised blessings.

Today is a new season for God's chosen people!

He is calling forth a new prophetic generation – a new breed of people.

When God dealt with Moses, He talked with him face to face. He didn't just talk to Moses in a presence he couldn't see. God **manifested** Himself.

It is the intimacy of this relationship with God that will bring about the manifestation of who He is.

In this new season, God is calling unto Himself a holy, sanctified, prophetic end time people through whom He will manifest His power and glory as a witness to the world that He is God!

The word "season" means "a period of time that is characterized by a particular circumstance or phenomenon". In the natural world, we have seasons. There is a hunting season, when a person is given the legal right to hunt certain animals. There is a fishing season where you must get a fishing license to fish.

Now is the season **legally** for you and I to hunt down the enemy of our soul! There is nothing the enemy can do about it because God is giving us His spiritual timing.

This is your breakthrough season!

Now is the time to reap God's promised blessings – for your physical needs, family needs, and financial needs – for every need you may have.

God has bound Himself to you by the authority of His Word. Just as God bound Himself to Moses and the children of Israel and demonstrated His covenant of blessing and provision, He has bound Himself to release His blessing and provision into your life.

The children of Israel were a marked people. The world saw God's hand of blessing was upon them. They saw how He delivered their enemies into their hands. They saw how He blessed and multiplied their crops, their offspring, their livestock and everything they possessed.

They saw and they trembled because God's chosen people served the living God who supernaturally manifested Himself on their behalf and poured out His blessings upon them. First, His

manifestation was through visitation to those whom He called to lead the people directly in their circumstances. He wanted to show them that He is God and there is no other god to be worshipped besides Him.

This is the season when God is once again going to manifest Himself upon His chosen people in supernatural provision and blessing as a witness to the world.

He is calling forth and marking an end-time prophetic generation. In the late seventies, God gave me this prophecy concerning another marked people:

"Once again before the coming of Jesus Christ, God will have a people who will be clearly marked. The whole world will tremble at those people before the coming of the Lord."

"The world doesn't fear the Church today. The world mocks the Church. The world laughs and ridicules the Church. But those days will soon be over."

"Before the coming of Jesus…and He's coming very soon…God's people will rise up in a new relationship – a new dimension with the Jehovah of Abraham and Isaac and Jacob."

"The sign of the blessing of Almighty God will rest upon them in such a way that the whole world will fear them more than they ever feared the Jew."

Beloved, this is the season when this prophecy will be fulfilled in the lives of His children who will walk humbly before Him in faithfulness and obedience.

God wants to bring you into a new end-time covenant relationship with Him that will open the windows of Heaven and release His supernatural provision and blessing.

His purpose: So that you will be positioned to step into all that God has called and anointed you to do in this end-time hour.

It is my prayer that as you read this book, the Holy Spirit will reveal to you, as never before, that God has marked you for His blessing.

You are His child! And, He desires to release within your life the fullness of His blessings.

Rise up in faith to take possession of all that He has provided for you!

God's Servant,

Morris Cerullo

The Priestly Fatherly Blessing

And the LORD spake unto Moses, saying, Speak unto Aaron and unto his sons, saying, On this wise ye shall bless the children of Israel, saying unto them,

The LORD bless thee, and keep thee:
The LORD make his face shine upon thee, and be gracious unto thee:
The LORD lift up his countenance upon thee, and give thee peace.
And they shall put my name upon the children of Israel; and I will bless them.

Numbers 6:22-27

You Are Marked For God's Blessing

CHAPTER
1

GOD HAS MARKED YOU FOR HIS BLESSINGS!

As a child of God, He wants to bring you into a new dimension of His supernatural provision where the fullness of His blessings is flowing into your life!

The word "dimension" means the degree to which something extends. The extension of the degree that you and I want to rise has no height, no depth, no breadth, and no limit!

How far do you want to go?

As you receive this revelation, I believe God will release into your life a blessing unlike any blessing you have ever experienced.

This will be the ultimate blessing that God has for you as one of His children.

You are one of God's chosen people. God will fulfill His promises to the Jewish people, but God's chosen people today are those who have their hearts circumcised, not with a knife, but by the blood of Jesus!

Today, you are God's chosen!

God is going to have a people.

We are living in His end-time harvest time. One of the great things God is doing is raising up a very special people who will walk in obedience and experience the covenant blessing He promised Abraham.

The only way God ever intended to provide for His people was through the supernatural manifestation of His provision.

You are the BLESSED of the Lord!

God has provided an unlimited reservoir of His riches that he wants to release in your life.

A reservoir is where water is stored for a purpose. I believe God has been storing up a reservoir of the rivers of His blessing and He is preparing to release it upon His people.

He has promised to rain down "showers" of His blessings upon His people.

God spoke through the prophet Ezekiel, *"And I will make them and the places round about My hill a blessing; and I will cause the showers to come down in their season; there shall be showers of blessing (of good insured by God's favor)." (Ezekiel 34:26, AMP)*

This is the greatest insurance policy in the world - the favor of God upon your life!

 You are marked for the outpouring of the blessing of Almighty God!

Are you ready for God to rain down showers of His blessing into the barren places of your life?

For a moment focus on the most barren, parched places of your life; in your body, your family, finances or ministry. God wants to pour His blessing into every barren place until all your needs are met.

When you make up your mind to walk in obedience before God, you will not be able to escape this blessing. It will not be necessary for you to search for it or run after it. It will run after you because it is God's commanded blessing upon His people.

God desires to pour His blessings upon you in such measure that you will not have room enough to contain them. He promises that when you bring your tithe into His storehouse He will release His blessing upon you to such a degree you will not be able to contain it!

"Test me in this," says the Lord Almighty, "and see if I will not throw open the floodgates of heaven and pour out so much blessing that you will not have room enough for it." (Malachi 3:10, NIV)

Floodgates control the height and flow of water. Their purpose is to hold the water in the reservoir until it gets full. When the water rises to flood level, the floodgates restrain and hold back the outburst of floodwaters. When it gets full, if the floodgates are not opened, they will break and overflow.

God says, "I will throw it open. I will release the river and take off the restraints. Everything that holds back My glory - My blessings, I will take off the limits!

God is unlocking the floodgates!

God's blessings are stored up for you behind the mighty floodgates ready to burst forth, and He has promised to throw back the floodgates of Heaven and release the floodwaters of His blessings upon you!

This is God's end-time!

Jesus is coming!

Nothing can hold back the blessings He has for your life!

Are you ready to receive them?

The Apostle Paul spoke of the "unsearchable riches" of Christ. He said, *"To me, though I am the very least of all the saints (God's consecrated people), this grace (favor, privilege) was granted and graciously entrusted: to proclaim to the Gentiles the unending (boundless, fathomless, incalculable and exhaustless) riches of Christ-wealth which no human being could have searched out." (Ephesians 3:8, AMP)*

Unending, boundless, fathomless, incalculable, exhaustless riches belong to you. Why? You are a child of God and He has marked you for His blessings.

Are you ready to receive a blessing unlike any blessing you have ever received - that which no amount of money can buy?

Do you have any idea what God has stored up for you? He is just holding it, waiting for the appointed time.

I believe with every fiber of my being that this is God's appointed time.

The riches of God's blessings He has stored up are immeasurable, unlimited and totally beyond our natural understanding!

They are all encompassing and so vast it is impossible to exhaust them!

You are a child of God, and He has marked you for His blessing. This is not a natural manifestation. God has marked you for supernatural provision.

That is why the Apostle Paul prayed for God to give the Ephesians the spirit of wisdom and revelation in the knowledge of Christ, and that their spiritual eyes would be opened.

Paul prayed:

> *(For I always pray) the God of our Lord Jesus Christ, the Father of Glory, that he may grant you a spirit of wisdom and revelation - of insight into mysteries and secrets - in the (deep and intimate) knowledge of Him, By having the eyes of your heart flooded with light, so that you can know and understand the hope to which He has called you and how rich is His glorious inheritance in the saints - His set-apart ones. And (so that you can know and understand) what is the immeasurable and unlimited and surpassing greatness of His power in and for us who believe, as demonstrated in the working of His might strength."*
>
> *Ephesians 1:17-19, AMP*

GOD WANTS TO BLESS YOU WITH
ALL THAT HE HAS AND IS!

The reason why God wants to pour His blessing upon you is because you are His child.

God does not want to hold back anything from His people. God gave birth to the Church and as a child of God, He does not want to hold back one thing of what He is.

He is our heavenly Father. He delights to release anything that He has and everything that He is to us.

The word "blessing" has been used so often that it has become commonplace and has lost its meaning. Many times we glibly say, "God bless you" or, "The Lord bless you" without really thinking of the full significance of what we are saying. There is no power behind what we are saying, because the meaning has been lost.

We often talk of the blessing of the Lord that was upon Abraham and the children of Israel, but what about God's blessing upon His people today?

When we refer to the "blessing" God wants to release in our lives, what do we really mean?

The word "bless" in the Old Testament is translated from the Hebrew word "barak". It is used over 300 times in the Old Testament. The word "blessing" is translated from the Hebrew word "berakah," which means, "to bless...to release prosperity."

When expressed by man, a "blessing" was a prayer for a blessing with the promise that was to come in the future. It was not a glib familiarity. It was a prayer and with that prayer came a promise. "Berakah" is also used to refer to God's blessing pronounced upon men by God's delegated spiritual authority. The promise was this: You are now marked for the blessing of God. In the future, as you speak the word of blessing under God's authority, something will be released.

Don't ever say, "God bless you" to someone unless you understand what you are saying, who you are speaking to, and recognize that God has given you the authority to release something into that person's life.

To have the blessing of the Lord upon your life means to be blessed in every possible way!

 God's blessing is His supernatural power that He imparts to His people through which He pours out His abundance into our lives.

EVERYTHING that God has, He wants to pour into your life! Why? Because you are His child!

God's blessing is much greater than just the accumulation of the world's wealth. Many people have acquired the riches of this world. They have wealth but not God's blessing. Along with their wealth, they have also acquired many sorrows. There is a continual striving and worry concerning how to keep their riches and acquire more.

God's blessing brings true riches. *"It is the blessing of the Lord that makes rich, and He adds no sorrow to it. "* (Proverbs 10:22, NAS) When God blesses and prospers His people with wealth, there is no worry or concern connected with it because they know God is their Source. *"But thou shalt remember the Lord thy God for it is he that giveth thee power to get wealth, that he may establish his covenant which he sware unto thy fathers, as it is this day."* (Deuteronomy 8:18) Knowing that it is His blessing, they are at peace.

GOD'S BLESSING MEANS
TOTAL WELL-BEING!

God's blessing upon your life is everything God has to offer...salvation, healing, deliverance, strength, provision, abundance, victory over your enemies, wisdom, revelation knowledge and understanding.

The blessing God wants to impart and release into your life is UNLIMITED! It is not limited to just one area of your life. It is not just limited to your finances. This supernatural blessing of the Lord involves **every area of your life**! It means that you are blessed by God in every possible way!

It means **total well being**! God desires His blessing to be upon your physical body and that sickness and disease be removed from you!

God has said, *"...I am the Lord that healeth thee."* (*Exodus 15:26*)

He is the God who heals all our diseases! *"Bless the Lord, O my soul, and forget not all his benefits: Who forgiveth all thine iniquities; who healeth all thy diseases."* (*Psalm 103:2-3*)

God desires to release His unlimited blessings upon you!

God desires that you be **blessed** spiritually...redeemed and cleansed from all sin...baptized with the Holy Spirit...the power of the Holy Spirit flowing through you...the fruit and gifts of the Spirit manifested in your life.

God has promised: *"For this is the covenant that I will make with the house of Israel after those days, saith the Lord; I will put my laws into their mind, and write them in their hearts: and I will be to them a God, and they shall be to me a people. (Hebrews 8:10) "And it shall come to pass afterward, that I will pour out my spirit upon all flesh; and your sons and your daughters shall prophesy, your old men shall dream dreams, your young men shall see visions."* (*Joel 2:28*)

God desires to bless your finances...to prosper and bless you with an increase...to bless all the work of your hands and everything you set your hand to do.

God has promised: *"And ye shall eat in plenty, and be satisfied, and praise the name of the Lord your God, that hath dealt wondrously with you: and my people shall never be ashamed." (Joel 2:26)*

He wants to pour out His abundance into your life so that all your needs will be met, and you will have an overabundance…a surplus that you will be able to sow into the Kingdom of God around the world.

God has promised: *"And God is able to make all grace (every favor and earthly blessing) come to you in abundance, so that you may always and under all circumstances and whatever the need, be self-sufficient - possessing enough to require no aid or support and furnished in abundance for every good work and charitable donation." (2 Corinthians 9:8, AMP)*

God desires that His blessing of divine protection be upon you and your family…that you be guarded and protected by His great power!

God has promised you: *"Fear thou not; for I am with thee: be not dismayed; for I am thy god: I will strengthen thee; yea, I will help thee; yea, I will uphold thee with the right hand of my righteousness." (Isaiah 41:10)*

God desires to **bless** you with His divine favor. David said, *"For surely, O Lord, you bless the righteous; you surround them with your favor as with a shield." (Psalm 5:12, NIV)*

God will bless you with His peace in every possible circumstance or situation you may face. *"The LORD will give strength unto his people; the LORD will bless his people with peace." (Psalm 29:11)*

God's blessing upon your life has a two-fold purpose:

> 1. God wants to pour His unlimited blessings
>   into your life because He wants you to know
>   His great love for you.

2. He wants His blessings to flow **through you** to the world around you so that the people of the world will know His great love for them.

When we seek God's blessings, we must not selfishly desire to have blessing after blessing heaped upon our lives just so that we can enjoy them for ourselves. We need God to make us a "channel of blessing" through which His blessings will flow freely to meet the needs of a lost and dying world.

GOD HAS SAID, "I WILL BLESS YOU!"

Before you can walk in the fullness of God's blessing upon your life, you must have a fresh revelation of God's great love and desire to lavish His blessings upon you.

We are not blessed simply because we go around claiming, "I am blessed!" We are blessed because a sovereign God desires to bless us and He has made every provision to release his blessings into our lives. God has so much blessing; He loves to pour it out.

God has always desired to have a people upon whom He could pour out His **blessing**. His first words to Adam and Eve were words of blessing:*"And God blessed them, and God said unto them, Be fruitful, and multiply, and replenish the earth, and subdue it: and have dominion over the fish of the sea, and over the fowl of the air, and over every living thing that moveth upon the earth. (Genesis 1:28)*

God created a beautiful garden, filled it with lush green grass, beautiful flowers of every color and variety, animals, trees, herbs, vegetables, a crystal clear river of water, and provided everything they needed. There was no sin, pain, sickness, disease or death. Then, he placed Adam and Eve in the Garden of Eden and gave them dominion and authority over the earth.

God blessed them and then He gave them authority to release the blessing. He told them to be fruitful and subdue the earth.

9

They were blessed in every possible way. They had need of nothing.

This was God's intention from the very beginning. It has not changed!

 God has made every provision to release His blessings upon His children.

God is going to have a people!

We are in God's end-time harvest-time cycle. One of the major points in this cycle is that God is separating a people from denominational, religious systems. And He is calling them out to be a separate people - a holy people - an obedient people.

He is calling forth a people to walk in His ways on a higher level with a greater intensity, sense of destiny and manifestation of all that He is and all that He has.

Why?

So that the world will know there is a living God - the same God of Israel!

God pronounced His blessing upon Noah: *"And God blessed Noah and his sons, and said unto them, Be fruitful, and multiply, and replenish the earth." (Genesis 9:1)*

God imputed authority to Noah and his sons. He gave them dominion over the earth. God told Noah, *"Everything that lives and moves will be food for you. Just as I gave you the green plants, I now give you everything." (Genesis 9:3, NIV)*

God blessed and multiplied Noah and his sons throughout the generations until they were spread throughout the earth.

God placed His hand of blessing upon Abraham. He chose Abraham to be the Father of a mighty nation and through him, He planned to bless the entire world.

God promised Abraham: *"And I will make of thee a great nation, and I will **bless** thee, and make thy name great; and thou shalt be* *a **blessing**: And I will **bless** them that **bless** thee, and curse him that curseth thee: and in thee shall all families of the earth be **blessed**." (Genesis 12:2-3)*

During this divine encounter, God revealed His great desire to bless not only Abraham and his descendents, but through his seed to bless all the nations upon the earth. God told Abraham, "...I will bless thee, and make thy name great."

Through the blessing of the Lord upon Abraham's life, he was **blessed in every way**. *"ABRAHAM WAS now old and well advanced in years, and the Lord had blessed him in every way." (Genesis 24:1, NIV)* The Lord had given him flocks, herds, camels, gold, silver, and servants. God had greatly multiplied all that he had until he was a rich man. *"And Abram was very rich in cattle, in silver, and in gold." (Genesis 13:2)*

In fact, God had so blessed Abraham and his nephew, Lot that their possessions were too great for them to live in the same area. *"But Lot, who went with Abram, also had flocks and herds and tents. Now the land was not able to nourish and support them so they might dwell together, for their possessions were too great for them to live together." (Genesis 13:5-6, AMP)*

God intends this blessing to be passed down through you to the next generation. Our problem is we think, "I grew up. I made it on my own. When my children grow up, they're on their own." Nothing could be more unscriptural.

God never intended for us to raise our children and throw them out saying, "Now that you are of age, you are on your own. Papa made it. Mama made it. Now, you make it."

God's intention was that the mature father and mother were to be so blessed of God that it overflowed onto their children and grand children! Don't be stingy! Stop holding back the inheritance! Let your kids see it now and be blessed by it.

The only people you spoil are people that walk in disobedience. You do not give, even to children, if they are disobedient. You give to them because they are obedient. You bless them and let it flow!

11

God does not want to hold His blessings back from you. You
cannot escape them. If you are obedient, His blessings will come!
They will flow! No power in hell or on earth can hold them back!

CHAPTER
2

GOD'S BLESSING IS FOREVER SETTLED IN THE HEAVENS!

When Abraham was ready to offer up Isaac, God called to him out of heaven and stopped him. There on the mountain, God confirmed His promise to Abraham of His blessing. He sealed it with His oath. *"...By myself have I sworn, saith the LORD, for because thou hast done this thing, and hast not withheld thy son, thine only son: That in blessing I will bless thee, and in multiplying I will multiply thy seed as the stars of heaven, and as the sand which is upon the sea shore; and thy seed shall possess the gate of his enemies."* (Genesis 22:16-17)

Notice that God said, "in blessing I will bless thee," and "in multiplying I will multiply thy seed." The double use of the words "bless", "blessing", "multiply" and "multiplying" in these verses are for special added emphasis. There was no question...no uncertainty...no doubt whatsoever that God would do what He promised.

In order to further show to those who would inherit His promise the unchangeableness of His divine purpose, God swore by Himself since there was none greater by whom He could swear, *"For when God made a promise to Abraham, because he could*

13

swear by no greater, he sware by himself, Saying, Surely blessing I will bless thee, and multiplying I will multiply thee." (Hebrews 6:13-14)

It was not necessary for God to swear by an oath. Whatever He speaks will come to pass! It is impossible for God to lie. *"God is not a man, that he should lie; neither the son of man, that he should repent: hath he said, and shall he not do it? or hath he spoken, and shall he not make it good? (Numbers 23:19)*

However, in His great desire to remove every trace of doubt in our minds concerning His purpose to pour His blessing upon us, He sealed His promise of blessing with His oath. *"Men indeed swear by a greater (than themselves), and with them in all disputes the oath taken for confirmation is final - ending strife. Accordingly, God also, in His desire to show more convincingly and beyond doubt, to those who were to inherit the promise, the unchangeableness of His purpose and plan, intervened (mediated) with an oath." (Hebrews 6:16-17, AMP)*

 God got between faith and doubt, and removed doubt so that faith could prevail.

The blessing of God is forever settled!

God was willing to put everything that He has and is on the line.

By doing this, He was saying, "There is no doubt that it will happen. You can stake your life and faith on the fact that I have sealed it.

Nobody can take this blessing from you. No ungodly influence around you can take it away from you.

God swore an oath and doubled the blessing upon Abraham. He said, "In blessing, I will bless you. In multiplying, I will multiply you."

It is God's desire that every trace of doubt be removed out of your mind concerning His promise to bless you. That is why He sealed the promise of His blessing with an oath. It was not necessary for Him to do it, but He did it for your sake so that you will have no doubt.

BEYOND DOUBT!

God wants you to know that just as he poured His blessings upon Abraham, that He desires to release His blessing upon you, your family and everything that belongs to you.

He has marked you for His blessings. He has given you His Word. He has said, "I **will** bless you!" He has sealed His Word with an oath. All possible margin for error has been removed. It is forever settled in the heavens!

The whole purpose and plan of God in presenting His blessing is to let us know we do not have to struggle for it.

HOW WOULD YOU LIKE TO HAVE
GOD'S HUNDRED-FOLD BLESSING?

God pronounced His blessing upon Isaac. He said, *"Sojourn in this land, and I will be with thee, and will bless thee: for unto thee, and unto thy seed, I will give all these countries, and I will perform the oath which I sware unto Abraham thy father; (Genesis 26:3)*

Look at the blessing God poured out upon Isaac. *"Then Isaac sowed in that land, and received in the same year an hundredfold: and the LORD blessed him." (Genesis 26:12)* God's blessing was so great upon Isaac that the very same year Isaac sowed his seed, he also received a hundred-fold increase.

How would you like the blessing of the Lord upon your life to be so great that you would receive one hundred times more than the amount you sowed?

Isaac *sowed* in a time of famine. The only thing God can bless is what we put in His hands. He can only bless what we release. Whatever you are willing to sow means whatever you are willing to entrust into God's hands.

The devil is not in control of the circumstances of your life.

15

God is in control.

If you release your life to Him, there is nothing that can come into your life, whether it is pain, shipwreck, persecution or misunderstanding, unless it comes by the permission of God Almighty, Who *is* in control.

 God has said, "I will bless you."
He will fulfill all His promises to you.

God told Isaac, "I will bless you!" I will perform the oath I sware to Abraham!"

In a time of great famine, God prospered Isaac to such a great extent he was known throughout the land. *"The man became rich, and his wealth continued to grow until he became very wealthy. He had so many flocks and herds and servants that the Philistines envied him. (Genesis 26:13-14, NIV)*

God had so multiplied and increased all that he had that Abimilech, the King of the land told Isaac, *"...Move away from us; you have become too powerful for us." (Genesis 26:16, NIV)*

Later King Abimilech and the chief captain of his army went to Isaac to enter into a treaty with him because they were afraid of him. They recognized that God's blessing was upon Isaac. They told Isaac: *"...We saw certainly that the LORD was with thee: and we said, Let there be now an oath betwixt us; even betwixt us and thee, and let us make a covenant with thee; That thou wilt do us no hurt, as we have not touched thee; and as we have done unto thee nothing but good, and have sent thee away in peace: thou art now the blessed of the LORD." (Genesis 26:28-29)*

God's blessing was so evident upon Isaac's life that even a heathen king recognized it and told Isaac, "You are the blessed of the Lord!"

God has marked you for His blessings! Why? Because you are His child.

God never intended His blessing to stop. He intended it to be transferred from generation to generation until it hit **this** dead, dry, lukewarm, compromising church.

JACOB WRESTLED FOR GOD'S BLESSING

The blessing of God was Upon Isaac's son, Jacob. God poured out His blessings upon him until he *"...became exceedingly rich, and had many sheep and goats, and maidservants, menservants, camels, and donkeys." (Genesis 30:43, AMP)*

Jacob could have been the most miserable man in the world, living under a heavy bondage because of what happened to him in taking Esau's birthright.

God intended for Jacob to have the birthright. There are no accidents with God.

Do you know what kept Jacob!

Heavenly visitations.

He would have been the most miserable man on earth, living under every kind of bondage and natural enslavement to the condemnation of his mind.

But, angels came. Not once, but twice. And God Himself spoke to him. Jacob wrestled with the Angel of the Lord and refused to let him go until He pronounced a blessing upon him. Jacob said, *"...I will not let You go unless You declare a blessing upon me." (Genesis 32:26, AMP)* The Angel of the Lord changed Jacob's name from Jacob (supplanter) to Israel (contender with God).

When Jacob asked him his name, the Angel of the Lord answered, *"...Why is it that you ask My name? And (the Angel of God declared) a blessing on (Jacob) there." (Genesis 32:29, AMP)*

Jacob fought battles just like you and I fight battles. Do you know why? We try to work out circumstances through our natural minds. It is so hard to let go.

When people have problems with their children, they think they need to talk until they are blue in the face. It is only after they talk, talk, talk, that they sit back in exasperation and say, "I just don't know. I've done my best but all my talking did not do any good."

Jacob had a conflict with his brother, Esau. In spite of the blessing, in spite of the riches, in spite of the angels of God coming and speaking to him, his heart was filled with fear.

Have you ever faced such an insurmountable circumstance that you were filled with fear?

Jacob was afraid Esau was going to kill him! He sent members of his household out to meet Esau. When they returned they brought a message. They said, "Esau is coming and he has 400 mighty men of valor!"

When Jacob heard this, it sent shock waves of fear through him. Jacob said, "God, what am I going to do now?" He forgot about the angel he had talked with earlier.

Jacob organized all of his people into bands. He said, "I'm going to make two bands of people. The first band will go with sheep, cattle, and lots of my wealth. The second band will go with lots more wealth. And the first thing I want you to do is bow."

Do you see what circumstances can do to you when you do not see them as they are?

 God wants you to see your circumstances, not according to the natural but as He sees them.

Jacob said, "If they kill you, then I'll come and bow down before Esau."

If only Jacob would have trusted what the angel had said!

Jacob, don't you remember the promise of your father? Don't you remember what God told him? When the blessing was given to you (even though you stole it), don't you remember God's promise that your brother would serve you?

God had to send the angel back again. The angel said, "I've got to really do a number on this guy. He doesn't understand. He doesn't even know who he is."

Jacob and the angel wrestled all night long. Finally, the angel got tired. You would have thought Jacob would have become tired.

The angel said to Jacob, "Let me go." You would have thought a supernatural being could have thrown Jacob aside. But, he couldn't.

Jacob said, "I'm not going to let you go until you bless me."

The angel asked Jacob his name. He answered, "My name is Jacob." The angel told him, "You are not the conniver you think you are. I have come to give you a revelation. Your name is no longer Jacob, but Israel. Do you know why I cannot leave you until I bless you? Because you have power with God and with men and you prevail! I cannot leave you until I bless you!"

If you could see as God sees, you would learn never to question.

You see, Esau was not coming to kill Jacob. God had already gone ahead and dealt with Esau's heart. He was coming to fall down before Jacob and confess that he was the blessed one of God.

Jacob could not see as God sees.

If we could only see as God sees concerning the circumstances of our lives and the things we go through, we would never question.

Do you know what removes questioning?

It is when you go through an experience where you failed to trust and found out that all your frustration and anxiety were for nothing. You learned you did not have to go through it. As a result, you are strengthened and the next time, you know.

THIS IS YOUR SEASON!

Beloved, you have a new name!

"Therefore if any man be in Christ, he is a new creature: old things are passed away; behold, all things are become new." (2 Corinthians 5:17)

Jesus said, *"...To him that overcometh will I give to eat of the hidden manna, and will give him a white stone, and in the stone a new name written, which no man knoweth saving he that receivedth it. (Revelation 2:17)*

God does not see me as Morris Cerullo.

He does not see you according to your earthly name.

19

He now sees you as one who has inherited the blessing of Abraham.

You are the one who has inherited all the blessings, through Jesus Christ, that God gave the people of Israel.

You are now His child!

You bear His Name!

Jacob had an encounter with God and God pronounced His blessing upon him. He named the place Peniel, meaning *"the face of God." Jacob said, "...For I have seen God face to face, and my life is spared and not snatched away." (Genesis 32:30, AMP)*

The Lord appeared to Jacob a second time and declared a blessing over him. God told Jacob, *"...I am God Almighty. Be fruitful and multiply; a nation and a company of nations shall come from you, and kings shall be born of your stock; the land which I gave Abraham and Isaac I will give to you; and to your descendents after you I will give the land. Then God ascended from him in the place where He talked with him." (Genesis 35:11-13, AMP)*

I believe the time is coming where God's people, who have dedicated themselves to walking in obedience to Him, can expect heavenly visitations.

God is not a respecter of persons. Too long the Church has just been an organized structure. Remember the prophecy God used me to give stating that the whole structure of the Church will be shaken. God is calling people out and He is going to give heavenly visitations. He is going to send angels to talk to people.

The God who manifested His supernatural power for Israel will, in His end-time work, manifest Himself again to His people! It is time for God to send heavenly messengers to His people to speak His message and demonstrate His Presence and glory in an unprecedented manner.

CHAPTER
3

GOD INTENDS FOR YOU
TO LIVE IN HIS FAVOR!

Are you ready to have God's unlimited blessings released in your life?

God's blessing was upon the Israelites when he supernaturally delivered them out of Egypt. God told Moses, "...*I will give this people favor and respect in the sight of the Egyptians; and it shall be that when you go, you shall not go empty-handed." (Exodus 3:21, AMP) "And the Lord gave the people favor in the sight of the Egyptians. Moreover the man Moses was exceedingly great in the land of Egypt, in the sight of Pharaoh's servants and of the people." (Exodus 11:3, AMP)*

When the Israelites left Egypt, they did not leave empty-handed. God filled their hands with the gold and silver of Egypt. His blessing was upon every household. There was not one feeble person among the tribes! "*He brought out Israel, laden with silver and gold, and from among their tribes no one faltered." (Psalm 105:37, NIV)*

The wealth of the sinner is laid up for the just! "*A good man leaveth an inheritance to his children's children: and the wealth of the sinner is laid up for the just." (Proverbs 13:22)*

Are you ready for it?

People do not give up their gold, silver, and precious jewels and things they love very easily. And, they do not give them up because they want to.

God was getting ready to lead almost three million Jews out of the land of bondage and He did not want them to go out broke. They worked as slaves for many years and God was going to be sure that they got their reward because they were His children.

God gave the people **favor**. He was working on the Egyptians and He gave Israel favor in the sight of the Egyptians. Every need was met. He not only gave them gold and silver, He gave them a mass healing miracle. Every one of them was healed. There wasn't one sick person among them. They had to walk, cross a sea, and enter into a wilderness. Before they got there, there was not a feeble person in their ranks.

God could have just led the children of Israel out of the land of Egypt and brought them across the Red Sea and into the wilderness. But, He did not do it. He did not do it until He gave them what was rightfully theirs.

God wants you to have His favor. He wants to give you what rightfully belongs to you. You do not have to beg for it. You do not have to struggle for it.

All you have to know is the key.

The key is that you are a child of God!

God wants to bring you into a new dimension of His supernatural provision where the fullness of His blessings will flow in your life.

YOU HAVE INHERITED THE
BLESSINGS OF ABRAHAM!

God's blessings were upon Moses and the children of Israel as they journeyed forty years, wandering in the wilderness. God supernaturally provided for them. Every need was met! During the forty years in the wilderness, their clothes and sandals did not wear out! (Deuteronomy 29:5)

The Lord spread a cloud for a covering [by day], and fire to give light in the night. The Israelites asked, and He brought quails, and satisfied them with the bread of heaven. He opened the rock, and waters gushed out; they ran in the dry places like a river. For he [earnestly] remembered His holy word and promise, and Abraham his servant. And he brought forth His people with joy, and His chosen with gladness and singing. And gave them the lands of the nations [of Canaan], and they reaped the fruits of those people's labor."
(Psalm 105:39-44, AMP)

At the end of the forty years, Moses told them, *"The LORD your God has blessed you in all the work of your hands. He has watched over your journey through this vast desert. These forty years the LORD your God has been with you, and you have not lacked anything. (Deuteronomy 2:7, NIV)*

It is time for the Abrahamic blessing to be ours!

I ask you, "Where is the God of Israel?"

Today we are God's chosen people. The Apostle Peter told the believers, *"But ye are a chosen generation, a royal priesthood; an holy nation, a peculiar people; that ye should show forth the praises of him who hath called you out of darkness into his marvellous light: which in time past were not a people: but are now the people of God..." (1 Peter 2:9-10)*

Paul told the believers in the church in Galatia, *"There is neither Jew nor Greek, there is neither bond nor free, there is neither male nor female: for ye are all one in Christ Jesus. And if ye be Christ's then are ye Abraham's seed, and heirs according to purpose." (Galatians 3:28-29)*

One who is a Jew today is one whose heart has been circumcised with the blood of Jesus. *"A man is not a Jew if he is only one outwardly, nor is circumcision merely outward and physical. No, a man is a Jew if he is one inwardly; and circumcision is*

25

circumcision of the heart, by the Spirit, not by the written code..." *(Romans 2:28-29, NIV)*

As a child of God, you are marked for God's blessings to be poured out upon you as God poured His blessings upon Israel.

God supernaturally fed His people with "the bread of heaven." No wonder there was not a feeble person among them! They were being fed supernaturally.

Let me ask you a couple of questions, "What are you eating?" "What are you putting inside your body?"

Many Christians today are filling themselves with fear, doubt, unbelief, criticism and faultfinding. The only way for you to be in health and be blessed is to be careful what you eat. Make sure it is "bread from heaven."

God did not leave the children of Israel on their own to fend for themselves. He was with them in the wilderness to provide for their every need. His blessings were upon them. When they entered the Promised Land God gave them houses, vineyards, crops and cities they did not even build.

Moses told the people:

> *"When the LORD your God brings you into the land he swore to your fathers, to Abraham, Isaac and Jacob, to give you - a land with large, flourishing cities you did not build, houses filled with all kinds of good things you did not provide, wells you did not dig, and vineyards and olive groves you did not plant - then when you eat and are satisfied, be careful that you do not forget the Lord, who brought you out of Egypt, out of the land of slavery."*
> *Deuteronomy 6:10-12, NIV*

The children of Israel did not have time to grow vineyards or to plant wheat.

But, they never lacked anything!

When they entered the Promised Land, God gave them houses, vineyards and crops.

He gave them cities they did not have to build. Not only did God transfer the wealth of Egypt to the Jew, He transferred the cities of the heathen into the hands of His people. This is a picture of the way God desires to bless His people today.

THE FLOODGATES
ARE READY TO OPEN!

God is going to have a people!

Are you ready for a new deeper life - a new covenant relationship with your Father through Christ?

Remember, it is the floodgates that store the water. When they rise to flood level, the gates are opened or they will burst.

God says, "Obey Me. Walk in obedience to me." *He tells us to test Him. "...Test me in this, says the* LORD *Almighty, "and see if I will not throw open the floodgates of heaven and pour out so much blessing that you will not have room enough for it." (Malachi 3:10, NIV)*

God is saying, "I am ready to let the waters of My blessing flow!"

Everything that God has stored up for us is going to break forth...

Uncontrollable...

Unquenchable...

An uncontainable flow of the river of God's blessing.

As the children of Israel prepared to enter the Promised Land, God promised to bless them above all other people. Moses told them, *"And he will love thee, and bless thee, and multiply thee: he will also bless the fruit of thy womb, and the fruit of thy land, thy corn, and thy wine, and thine oil, the increase of thy kine, and the flocks of thy sheep, in the land which he sware unto thy fathers to give thee...there shall not be male or female barren among you, or among your cattle." (Deuteronomy 7:13-14)*

In other words, God planned to pour out His blessings upon them, upon all that their hands touched, upon their possessions and bless them in every possible way!

God gave them a choice to walk in obedience to Him and have his blessings released in their lives, or to disobey and bring curses upon themselves. Moses told them, *"**Behold, I set before you this day a blessing and a curse; A blessing, if ye obey the commandments of the Lord your God, which I command you this day:** And a curse, if ye will not obey the commandments of the Lord your God..." (Deuteronomy 11:26-28)*

ARE YOU READY TO ENTER INTO GOD'S COMMANDED BLESSINGS?

Moses laid out all God's promised blessings and told the children of Israel, *"And all these blessings shall come on thee, **and overtake thee**, if thou shalt hearken unto the voice of the LORD thy God." (Deuteronomy 28:2)*

God said His blessings will overtake you! He is ready to bless you with a blessing unlike any blessing you have ever received.

*"**Blessed** shalt thou be in the city, and blessed shalt thou be in the field.*

***Blessed** shall be the fruit of thy body, and the fruit of thy ground, and the fruit of thy cattle, the increase of thy kine, and the flocks of thy sheep.*

***Blessed** shall be thy basket and thy store.*

***Blessed** shalt thou be when thou comest in, and blessed shalt thou be when thou goest out.*

The Lord shall cause thine enemies that rise up against thee to be smitten before thy face: they shall come out against thee one way, and flee before thee seven ways."

Deuteronomy 28:3-7

DO YOU WANT GOD'S BLESSINGS
TO RUN AFTER YOU?

God's blessings upon the children of Israel were dependent upon one thing: their covenant relationship with Him. As long as they loved Him with all their hearts and walked in obedience to Him and His commandments, they would live under His **commanded** blessings. It would not even be necessary for them to seek after them. God told them all His blessings would **overtake** them. His blessings would come after them and take hold of them!

Look at the blessing that was upon the children of Israel.

God's blessing was upon their children...

Upon their land...

Upon their crops...

Upon their livestock...

Upon everything they had!

Moses told them, *"And the Lord shall make you have a surplus of prosperity, through the fruit of your body, of your livestock, and of your ground, in the land which the Lord swore to your fathers to give you." (Deuteronomy 28:11, AMP)*

The blessing of the Lord was upon their storehouses, upon their increase, and upon all the work of their hands. They did not have to struggle to receive God's blessings; Moses told the people that God would **command** His blessing to come upon them.

How would you like to live under the commanded of God's blessings? It is coming if you will receive the word and act on it.

He said: "The LORD shall command the blessing upon thee in thy storehouses, and in all that thou settest thine hand unto..." (Deuteronomy 28:8) He told them: *"The LORD shall open unto thee his good treasure, the heaven to give the rain unto thy land in his season, **and to bless all the work of thine hand...**" (Deuteronomy 28:12)*

The blessing of the Lord was upon them wherever they went...in the city or in the field. Moses told them, *"Blessed shalt thou be in the city, and blessed shalt thou be in the field. Blessed shalt thou be when thou comest in, and blessed shalt thou be when thou goest out." (Deuteronomy 28:3,6)*

YOU CAN LIVE UNDER THE COMMANDED BLESSINGS OF GOD!

Just as God promised to bless the children of Israel in every possible way, as they were obedient to Him, He wants to release His blessing into your life, and for His blessings to remain upon you!

Beloved, today...believe you are the blessed of the Lord! You have inherited the blessing of God that was upon Abraham, Isaac, Jacob...that was upon Moses and the children of Israel.

Believe God has marked you. He has placed His Name on you to be blessed with all that He is and has!

The Apostle Paul said, *"Know ye therefore that they which are of faith, the same are the children of Abraham." (Galatians 3:7)* He said, *"So then they which be of faith are **blessed** with faithful Abraham." (Galatians 3:9)*

Through Christ, you are Abraham's seed, and have inherited the blessing of God! *"And if ye be Christ's, then are ye Abraham's seed, and heirs according to the promise." (Galatians 3:29)*

The word "heir" is translated from a Greek word meaning, "one who obtains a lot or portion, especially of an inheritance."

You do not have to struggle to receive God's blessings. You are a child of God...a joint-heir with Jesus!

God has placed His Name upon you, and you are the **blessed** of the Lord!

God has planned for His blessings to be so strong upon His people today that the people of the world will know we are the people He has blessed! *"And their offspring shall be known among the nations, and their descendants among the peoples. All who see them [in their prosperity] will recognize and acknowledge that they are the people whom the Lord has blessed." (Isaiah 61:9, AMP)*

Now, let's get down to where the "rubber meets the road!" God's Word from cover to cover reveals His desire and will to pour out His blessings upon His people.

Why aren't more Christians today living under the fullness of God's blessings upon their physical bodies, their finances, their families, their businesses and ministries?

You cannot earn or buy God's blessings. The key to the release of His blessings upon your life today is dependent upon one thing: your covenant relationship with God. You cannot expect to live under God's commanded blessings if you are not living in close covenant relationship with the Lord and are not walking in faith and obedience to Him.

As long as the children of Israel obeyed God and kept His commandments, they enjoyed His blessings. But, when they turned away from him and disobeyed, they brought cursing upon themselves instead of blessing.Through Christ, you are Abraham's seed, and have inherited the blessing of God! *"And if ye be Christ's, then are ye Abraham's seed, and heirs according to the promise."* *(Galatians 3:29)* There is only one condition to inherit God's blessings - that you are a child of God!

FAITH AND OBEDIENCE ARE THE KEYS TO REAPING GOD'S BLESSINGS!

You do not have to struggle to receive it. God's blessings legally belong to you as His child and as a Joint-heir with Jesus! However, it is not enough to know these blessings are yours. You can even agree with the Word God has spoken. The only way you will be able to actually take possession of your inheritance and have the fullness of the blessing of God flowing in your life is through faith and obedience.

God pronounced His blessings upon Abraham, Isaac, Jacob, Moses and the children of Israel but they were only able to take possession of those blessings as they received God's promise of blessing and acted in faith and obedience to what He had spoken.

31

An entire generation of the children of Israel failed to enter the Promised Land and take possession of all His promised blessings because of their unbelief.

> "Who were they who heard and rebelled? Were they not all those Moses led out of Egypt? And with whom was he angry for forty years? Was it not with those who sinned, whose bodies fell in the desert? And to whom did God swear that they would never enter his rest if not to those who disobeyed? So we see that they were not able to enter, because of their unbelief" Hebrews 3:16-19, NIV.

They refused to believe and were unable to take hold of God's blessings.

It is through faith and patience we are able to take hold of God's promised blessings. (Hebrews 6:12) Abraham took possession of God's promised blessings through his obedience, faith and patience. *"By faith Abraham, when he was called to go out into a place which he should after receive for an inheritance, obeyed;..."* (Hebrews 11:8) Abraham obeyed God. *"And so, after he had patiently endured, he obtained the promise."* (Hebrews 6:15) Abraham received the promised blessings of God because he did not question or doubt, but obeyed God.

God will command His blessings upon you, your children, and all the work of your hands!

Believe the Word of the Lord to you, and act in faith upon it. Do not walk around whining and complaining about your circumstances...your problems...your lack. Release your faith, believe and expect God to release His blessings upon you. Look for them to come running after you!

God has set His Name upon you. As His child, you are marked by God for His blessing to be released in your life. He is the source of all blessing. He has placed His Name on the line, and said, "I will bless you with all that is mine!"

As you release your faith:

EXPECT God's blessing of healing to be released upon you!

EXPECT God's blessing to be upon all the work of your hands!

EXPECT God's blessing to be upon your ministry!
EXPECT God to release His spiritual blessings upon you!
EXPECT God's blessing and protection to be upon you wherever you are!
EXPECT God's favor to be upon your life!
Begin to speak in faith,

"The Lord has placed His Name upon me and marked me for His blessing. I am the blessed of the Lord! His blessings are upon me and all that is mine. As I walk in obedience to Him, God has commanded His blessings to come upon me! By faith, I receive the blessings of the Lord upon me and my family!"

"There is neither Jew nor Greek, there is neither bond nor free, there is neither male nor female: for ye are all one in Christ Jesus. And if ye be Christ's, then are ye Abraham's seed, and heirs according to the promise." (Galatians 3:28-29)

"The Spirit itself beareth witness with our spirit, that we are the children of God: And if children, then heirs; heirs of God, and joint-heirs with Christ; if so be that we suffer with him, that we may be also glorified together." (Romans 8:16-17)

CHAPTER
4

YOU ARE THE BLESSED
OF THE LORD!

God has marked you with His Name and desires to bless you above all other people upon the earth.

Do you believe it?

Just as God chose the children of Israel, set them apart to be a special people unto Himself above all people upon the earth, and poured His blessings upon them, He has raised up a people today upon whom He has promised to pour out His blessings.

God has chosen us! We are a chosen generation, a royal priesthood, a holy nation. We are now the people of God called by his Name!

Do you believe it?

God has said, *"...I will live with them and walk among them, and I will be their God, and they will be my people." (2 Corinthians 6:16, NIV)* He promised to take us unto Himself and be a Father to us. *"...I will receive you, And will be a Father unto you, and ye shall be my sons and daughters, saith the Lord Almighty." (2 Corinthians 6:17-18)*

And, because we are His sons and daughters, we are heirs of God through Christ! (Galatians 7:7) Through Christ we have not only been redeemed from the curse, we have inherited the BLESSING OF ABRAHAM! All the blessings of God belong to us!

Christ became a curse for us, and has redeemed us from the curse of the law, *"That the blessing of Abraham might come on the Gentiles through Jesus Christ; that we might receive the promise of the Spirit through faith." (Galatians 3:14)* Through His death and resurrection, Christ not only broke the curse and power of Satan from our lives, He released the blessing of Abraham! The fullness of God's blessing has been released, but you must take it by faith!

God never intended for His blessings to stop with the children of Israel. He ordained His blessings be passed from generation to generation.

When God pronounced His blessing upon Abraham, he was not only speaking to Abraham but also to his seed.

The Lord promised to multiply Abraham's seed as the stars of heaven and as the sand upon the seashore. God told Abraham, *"And in thy seed shall all the nations of the earth be blessed..." (Genesis 22:18)*

God purposed in His heart to raise up a holy, righteous seed through which He would one day bring a Redeemer. It was through this seed that He would send His only Son to break the curse of sin and restore man into full fellowship with Him whereby His blessings were released into their lives.

God not only planned that Abraham and His seed would be blessed but that they would be the instruments through which His blessing flowed.

When God separated Israel to be His people and entered into a covenant with them, He became their Heavenly Father. He took them into family relationship! As their Father, He promised to pour His blessings upon them, upon everything they possessed and all the work of their hands.

Why?

Because as His children He desired them to be representatives of all He is!

He released His blessing upon them through those whom he had sanctified, anointed and delegated this authority. Moses, Aaron and the priests were appointed as God's spokesmen to the children of Israel and one of their major responsibilities was to release God's blessing upon the people.

God gave Moses specific instructions to give Aaron and his sons regarding releasing His blessing upon them.

The Lord said to Moses, *"Tell Aaron and his sons. 'This is how you are to bless the Israelites. Say to them: The Lord bless you and keep you; the Lord make his face shine upon you and be gracious to you; the Lord turn his face toward you and give you peace."* *(Numbers 6:22-26, NIV)*

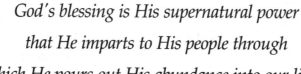

God's blessing is His supernatural power
that He imparts to His people through
which He pours out His abundance into our lives.

Aaron and his sons were consecrated to release God's blessing upon the children of Israel. *"...and Aaron was separated, that he should sanctify the most holy things, he and his sons for ever, to burn incense before the LORD, to minister unto him, and to bless in his name for ever."* *(1 Chronicles 23:13)*

When Moses, Aaron or the priests spoke under the authority of God, the people considered it as God speaking to them.

Acting in the Name and authority of The Father who commanded the blessing, the blessing carried with it a promise and the one speaking it invoked it with God's authority.

This act of blessing in the Name of the Lord God Almighty was not just a mere expression of good will or a simple prayer.

Invoking the covenant Name of God upon the people carried a tremendous significance. It released the power of all that is behind God's Name to fulfill the promised blessing.

The Name of God could not be used in blessing except by the one to whom God had given the authority. And, whether it was a prophet, priest or king it had to be by God's direction. With the Name of God pronounced in blessing, came the blessing, the favor and Presence of God to rest upon the individual.

AS THEIR FATHER, GOD RELEASED
HIS BLESSINGS UPON ISRAEL

After the altar was consecrated and anointed and Aaron and the priests had been consecrated as God had directed, Aaron offered up the sin offering, burnt offering and peace offerings on the altar. When he finished, he lifted up his hand toward the people and BLESSED them.

Then Moses went with Aaron into the tabernacle and when they came out, they BLESSED the people. *"And Moses and Aaron went into the tabernacle of the congregation, and came out, and blessed the people: and the glory of the LORD appeared unto all the people." (Leviticus 9:23)*

God manifested His awesome Presence among His people. His Shekinah glory came down! Fire came out from before the Lord and consumed the burnt offering. God wanted His people to know that He was with them and had accepted their sacrifice. When all the people saw this great manifestation, they shouted and fell prostrate on their faces before God. *"And there came a fire out from before the Lord, and consumed upon the altar the burnt offering and the fat: which when all the people saw, they shouted, and fell on their faces." (Leviticus 9:24)*

God promised to give Isaac and his seed the land He had promised Abraham. God promised Isaac, *"Sojourn in this land, and I will be with thee, and will bless thee: for unto thee, and unto thy seed, I will give all these countries, and I will perform the oath which I sware unto Abraham thy father: (Genesis 26:3)* He told Isaac: "I will be with you...I will bless you...I will perform my oath!" Isaac, in faith, released the blessing God had spoken over him to his son Jacob. *"By faith Isaac blessed Jacob and Esau concerning things to come." (Hebrews 11:20)*

When it came time for Isaac to release the blessing of God upon his firstborn, Esau, Jacob deceived him by pretending to be Esau to receive his blessing. (Genesis 27:15-26)

The birthright of the firstborn consisted of a double portion of what His father had to leave. He became head of the family, was in charge of the family property, and was responsible for the care of the younger sons, the widow and unmarried daughters. He also received the blessing, which placed him in a close and favored covenant relationship with God.

Jacob succeeded in taking both the birthright and blessing of Esau.

With God's Name pronounced in blessing comes the blessing, the favor and Presence of God.

Isaac pronounced God's blessing upon Jacob. He told him, *"May God give you of heaven's dew and of earth's richness—an abundance of grain and new wine. May nations serve you and peoples bow down to you. Be lord over your brothers, and may the sons of your mother bow down to you. May those who curse you be cursed and those who bless you be blessed." (Genesis 27:28-29, NIV)*

When Esau came to Isaac and discovered that Jacob had stolen his blessing; he wanted Isaac to bless him. Isaac told him that he had blessed Jacob. *"...I blessed him - and indeed he will be blessed." (Genesis 27:33, NIV)*

GOD'S BLESSING CANNOT BE BROKEN!

The supernatural blessing of God is invoked by speaking it aloud. Once the blessing has been spoken, it cannot be broken. God can stop it because of an individual's disobedience, but no man can stop it! That is why some people do not understand why some people who fail still have God's anointing, *"For the gifts and calling of God are without repentance." (Romans 11:29)*

Esau cried out, *"...Haven't you reserved any blessing for me?" (Genesis 27:36, NIV)*

Isaac answered, *"I have made him lord over you and have made all his relatives his servants, and I have sustained him with grain and new wine. So what can I possibly do for you, my son?" (Genesis 27:37, NIV)*

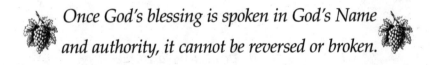

Once God's blessing is spoken in God's Name and authority, it cannot be reversed or broken.

Esau wept bitterly and said, *"...Do you have only one blessing, my father? Bless me too, my Father." (Genesis 27:38, NIV)*

Isaac answered, *"...Your dwelling will be away from the earth's riches, away from the dew of heaven above. You will live by the sword and you will serve your brother. But when you grow restless, you will throw his yoke from off your neck." (Genesis 27:39-40, NIV)*

Before sending Jacob to Paddan-aram to find a wife, Isaac called Jacob and released the blessing of Abraham upon him. Isaac told Jacob: *"May God Almighty bless you and make you fruitful and increase your numbers until you become a community of peoples. May he give you and your descendents the blessing given to Abraham..." (Genesis 28:3-4, NIV)*

Once the blessing of God was spoken in God's Name and authority over Jacob, it could not be reversed or stopped by any man! God was with Jacob and His commanded blessings came upon him. God multiplied and prospered him until he *"...became exceedingly rich, and had many sheep and goats, and maidservants, menservants, camels, and donkeys." (Genesis 30:43, AMP)*

GOD'S BLESSING WAS RELEASED FROM GENERATION TO GENERATION!

God never intended for His blessing to stop. Throughout the generations, His blessing was released to the people through those whom God had established as His delegated authority:

• Jacob blessed Joseph and his two sons, Manasseh and Ephraim.

> *"And he blessed Joseph, and said, God, Before whom my fathers Abraham and Isaac did walk, the God which fed me all my life long unto this day, The Angel which redeemed me from all evil, bless the lads; and let my name be named on them, and the name of my fathers Abraham and Isaac; and let them grow into a multitude in the midst of the earth.*
>
> *Genesis 48:15-16*

• Moses was blessed of the Lord. He was known as the "Friend" of God. He was God's spokesman and used mightily by God to do signs and wonders in delivering the children of Israel out of Egypt.

God blessed Moses with a long life and when he died, he was still full of strength and power.

> *"And Moses was an hundred and twenty years old when he died: his eye was not dim, nor his natural force abated."*
>
> *Deuteronomy 34:7*

Before he died, Moses pronounced blessing upon the twelve tribes of Israel. He said:

41

"Blessed are you, O Israel! Who is like you, a people saved by the LORD? He is your shield and helper and your glorious sword. Your enemies will cower before you, and you will trample down their high places."

Deuteronomy 33:29, NIV

• Joshua pronounced God's blessing upon Caleb.

"And Joshua blessed him, and gave unto Caleb the son of Jephunneh Hebron for an inheritance."

Joshua 14:13

• After David brought the Ark of the Covenant back to the city of David, he blessed the people in the Name of the Lord.

"And as soon as David had made an end of offering burnt offerings and peace offerings, he blessed the people in the name of the LORD of hosts."

2 Samuel 6:18

God's blessings were upon David. God was with him, gave him victory over his enemies, and made his name great upon the earth. God pronounced His blessing upon David. He sent the prophet Nathan to tell him:

"...thine house and thy kingdom shall be established forever before thee: thy throne shall be established for ever."

2 Samuel 7:16

Immediately, when David heard God's promise he went before the Lord and prayed.

"Therefore now let it please thee to bless the house of thy servant, that it may continue for ever

before thee: for thou, O Lord GOD hast spoken it:
and with thy blessing let the house of thy servant
be blessed for ever."

2 Samuel 7:29

• At the dedication of the Temple Solomon **blessed** the people.

"And he stood, and blessed all the congregation
of Israel with a loud voice, saying, Blessed be the
Lord, that hath given rest unto his people Israel,
according to all that he promised: there hath not
failed one word of all his good promise, which he
promised by the hand of Moses his servant.

1 Kings 8:55-56

• King Hezekiah cleansed the Temple, restored the worship and sacrificial offerings, and consecrated the Levites and priests to serve in the Temple as God had commanded. He called the children of Israel together to observe the Passover. At the celebration of the Passover the priests and Levites arose and **blessed** the people.

"Then the priests and Levites arose and blessed
the people: and their voice was heard, and their
prayer came up to his holy dwelling place, even
unto heaven."   *2 Chronicles 30:27*

GOD'S BLESSINGS ARE
UNCHANGEABLE AND IRREVERSIBLE!

The blessing is the supernatural power of God imparted into our lives when directed by God's delegated authority.

The blessing, once spoken becomes a reality. It cannot be reversed. When Barak, the King of Moab asked Balaam, the priest, to pronounce a curse upon the children of Israel, Balaam told him, *"How shall I curse, whom God hath not cursed? Or how shall I defy, whom the Lord hath not defied?"* (Numbers 22:8) Instead of speaking cursing, he blessed the children of Israel.

43

When Barak persisted, Balaam answered, *"God is not a man, that he should lie; neither the son of man, that he should repent: hath he said, and shall he not do it? or hath he spoken, and shall he not make it good? Behold, I have received commandment to bless: and he hath blessed; and I cannot reverse it." (Numbers 23:19-20)*

The blessing spoken by God to Abraham, Isaac and Jacob could not be broken! God had commanded His blessings upon the children of Israel and they were blessed. Balaam, the priest, as God's authority had been commanded by God to speak His blessings over them and there was nothing he nor the King of Moab could do to stop or reverse them.

Think about the significance of this to you today. Through Christ, the fullness of God's blessings has been released. He has not only redeemed you from the **curse** of the Law; He has transferred all the **blessings** God has to offer to you, including the Abrahamic Covenant blessing. *"That the blessing of Abraham might come on the Gentiles through Jesus Christ; that we might receive the promise of the Spirit through faith." (Galatians 3:14)*

 God's blessings are unchangeable and irreversible.

You are no longer living under a curse, but you are living under God's **commanded** blessings!

It is possible for you to walk out from under His blessings through your disobedience and unbelief, but there is nothing any man or Satan and all his principalities can do to stop his blessings upon your life. NOTHING!

They are unchangeable and irreversible!

As a child of the living God, redeemed by the blood of Jesus, he has placed His Name upon you and you are the blessed of the Lord!

"Blessed is the man who fears the Lord, who finds great delight in his commands. His children will be mighty in the land; the generation of the upright will be blessed. Wealth and riches are in his house, and his righteousness endures forever."

(Psalm 112:1-3, NIV)

YOU CAN LIVE UNDER THE COMMANDED BLESSINGS OF GOD!

Beloved, if you have not yet come into this experience, now is your time!

God has pronounced His blessing upon those who walk uprightly before Him. He has said, "They will be blessed!" He has promised that our children **will be** mighty and that wealth and riches will be in their house!

God's **commanded blessings** are upon all those who fear Him and walk in accordance with His word:

"BLESSED - HAPPY, fortunate (to be envied) - is every one who fears, reveres and worships the Lord; who walks in His ways and lives according to His commandments. For you shall eat (the fruit) of the labor of your hands; happy, blessed, fortunate (enviable) shall you be, and it shall be well with you. Your wife shall be as a fruitful vine in the innermost parts of your house; your children like olive plants round about your table. Behold, thus shall the man be blessed who reverently and worshipfully fears the Lord."

Psalm 128:1-4, AMP

Are you ready for this?

God's **commanded blessings** are upon those who love the Word and continually meditate upon His precepts:

> *"BLESSED IS the man who does not walk in the*
> *counsel of the wicked or stand in the way of sinners*
> *or sit in the seat of mockers. But his delight is in the*
> *law of the Lord and on his law he meditates day and*
> *night. He is like a tree planted by streams of water*
> *which yield fruit in its season and whose leaf does*
> *not wither. Whatever he does prospers."*
>
> *Psalm 1:1-3, NIV*

When you fill your heart and mind with the Word and with God's precepts, and keep them before you continually, the commanded blessing of God will be upon you. You will not become weary or barren and whatever you do will prosper!

Are you ready to live under the commanded blessings of God where everything you do has God's favor on it and prospers?

God's **commanded blessings** are upon those who seek Him with their whole heart:

> *"BLESSED, HAPPY, fortunate (to be envied) are*
> *the undefiled - the upright, truly sincere and*
> *blameless - in the way (of the revealed will of God)'*
> *who walk - that is order their conduct and*
> *conversation - in (the whole of God's revealed will)*
> *the law of the Lord. Blessed, happy, fortunate (to be*
> *envied) are they who keep His testimonies, and who*
> *seek, inquire for and of Him and crave Him with the*
> *whole heart. Yes, they do no unrighteousness - no*
> *willful wandering from His precepts; they walk in*
> *His ways."*
>
> *Psalm 119: 1-3, AMP*

CHAPTER
5

GOD HAS PLACED HIS NAME ON THE LINE

God has blessed us with unlimited spiritual blessings in the heavenly realms in Christ.

The Apostle Paul told the Ephesians, *"Praise be to the God and Father of our Lord Jesus Christ, who has blessed us in the heavenly realms with every spiritual blessing..." (Ephesians 1:3, NIV).*

The blessing of God has been released upon us through Christ. His blessing includes everything that God has and is. God has put His Name on the line and said, "I will bless you with all that is mine." (Galatians 3:8-9) To take hold of all His blessings, we must live according to His Word and act in faith.

It grieves my heart to see many Christians forfeiting God's blessings through their unbelief. The Father has released His commanded blessings upon them, but they fail to reach out and appropriate them in their lives because they do not understand all the blessings He has provided for them. Their eyes are so focused on their need...their circumstances...their problems that they fail to see God's provision.

Through Christ, we inherit the promised blessings of God by faith. Paul told the Galatians, *"...Just as no one can set aside or add to a human covenant that has been duly established, so it is in this case. The promises were spoken to Abraham and to his seed. The Scripture does not say, 'and to seeds,' meaning many people, but 'and to your seed,' meaning one person, who is Christ." (Galatians 3:15-16, NIV)*

It is clear that God's promised blessing to Abraham, sealed with His oath, was made to a Royal Seed, which is Christ. When Christ came, he came to remove the curse of the Law and to release God's blessing.

On the cross, He became a curse for us, thereby forever removing the curse of the Law from us. Paul said, *"Christ redeemed us from the curse of the law by becoming a curse for us, for it is written: 'Cursed is everyone who is hung on a tree.' " (Galatians 3:13, NIV)*

Christ became a curse for you so that you can inherit and live under God's blessing! He removed it from you - lifted it from your shoulders and brought you into the blessing of the Father. *"He redeemed us in order that the blessing given to Abraham might come to the Gentiles through Christ Jesus, so that by faith we might receive the promise of the Spirit." (Galatians 3:14, NIV)*

YOU ARE ABRAHAM'S SEED AND HAVE INHERITED THE FATHER'S BLESSING

It is **by faith** we receive Christ and become sons of God. And, it is **by faith** that we inherit the promise of God's Spirit and all His blessings!

Paul said, *"You are all sons of God through faith in Christ Jesus, for all of you who were baptized into Christ have clothed yourselves with Christ." (Galatians 3:26-27, NIV)*

As a result of belonging to Christ, you are also Abraham's seed and inherit the blessing! Paul said, *"If you belong to Christ, then you are Abraham's seed, and heirs according to the promise." (Galatians 3:29, NIV)*

The blessing is passed down from Jesus Christ to us!

Paul made it clear that the seed of Abraham is the people who actually live by faith. He said, *"Know and understand that it is [really] the people [who live] by faith who are [the true] sons of Abraham."* (Galatians 3:7, AMP) Those who are blessed are the ones who live by faith and take hold of God's promises. *"So then, those who are people of faith are blessed and made happy and favored by God [as partners in fellowship] with the believing and trusting Abraham."* (Galatians 3:9, AMP)

Christ has redeemed you from the curse

and brought you into the blessing

of the Father.

You are marked by God for His blessings!

By faith, you are saved and redeemed from the curse!

By faith, you are a child of God!

By faith, you belong to a Royal Seed - to Christ!

By faith, you enter into the Holy of Holies and take hold of everything you need!

As a child of God, He has placed His Name upon you and marked you for His blessing!

THROUGH CHRIST, THE FULLNESS OF GOD'S BLESSING HAS BEEN RELEASED UPON YOU!

God released His blessings upon the children of Israel through Moses, Aaron and through those, He gave His authority. The blessing was invoked by speaking it aloud. As they pronounced God's blessing, in God's authority and in His Name, it was the same as if God were speaking it.

As they invoked the blessing, they stood before the people with their hands lifted and outstretched and their faces toward the

51

people. *"And Aaron lifted up his hand toward the people, and blessed them,..." (Leviticus 9:22)*

As our Great High Priest, Christ, acting on behalf of the Father released the fullness of His blessings upon the Church.

Christ offered Himself as the one perfect sacrifice to redeem and restore us into fellowship with God. On the cross, he became a curse for us. He lifted the curse of the Law from us.

By his own blood he entered into the Holy of Holies and obtained our salvation. He bought us with His blood! *"Neither by the blood of goats and calves, but by his own blood he entered in once into the holy place, having obtained eternal redemption for us." (Hebrews 9:12)*

The Father accepted His sacrifice and raised Him from the dead. He exalted Christ to a position of supreme power and authority over all things. *"Therefore God exalted him to the highest place and gave him the name that is above every name, that at the name of Jesus every knee should bow, in heaven and on earth and under the earth, and every tongue confess that Jesus Christ is Lord, to the glory of God the Father." (Philippians 2:9-11, NIV)*

In this position of supreme power and authority, before He ascended into heaven, Christ lifted up His hands and released the blessing of Almighty God!

Can you see Him standing there on the hillside as our Great High Priest with His hands outstretched toward His disciples and followers? *"And he led them out as far as to Bethany, and he lifted up his hands, and blessed them. And it came to pass, while he blessed them, he was parted from them, and carried up into heaven." (Luke 24:50-51)*

The first thing the Father did in His relationship with Adam and Eve was to release blessing. The last thing Jesus, our Great High Priest, did was to release the Father's blessing!

The Father has released His blessing upon you. It cannot be changed or reversed.

There is no man, Satan nor all his principalities that can stop God's blessings from coming upon your life.

You are the blessed of the Lord!

The choice is up to you.

Through faith and obedience, you can walk under the commanded blessings of God whereby all the blessings he has provided are flowing into your life.

See Christ, your Great High Priest, with His hands outstretched to you today, invoking and releasing the fullness of the blessing of the Father into your life.

Reach out to Him right now and receive it by faith!

As a step and expression of your faith say aloud:

"I am marked by God. He has placed His Name
upon me and marked me for His blessing.
Through Christ, the fullness of God's blessing
has been released upon me and I am blessed!
Nothing can stop God's blessing from my life.
By faith, I will walk under
God's commanded blessings!"

CHAPTER
6

YOU ARE MARKED BY GOD'S NAME TO RECEIVE ALL THAT HE HAS

Knowing that Christ has released the fullness of God's blessings upon His Church, the question that arises in the hearts of many Christians today is, "How can I live under the commanded blessings of God?"

Some look at their circumstances: their financial struggles, their battle against sickness, family problems and their lack in different areas of their life and wonder, "Why don't I have the blessings of God flowing into my life?" "I believe it is God's will to bless me, but I do not see His blessings being poured out upon my finances, upon my children, upon my business." "How do I take hold of God's blessings and appropriate them in my life?"

One of the major reasons many Christians are not experiencing the fullness of the blessings God has provided is because they do not understand the provision of God's blessing for their lives. So many are living below what God has for them because of their lack of knowledge. God said, "*My people are destroyed for lack of knowledge...*" *(Hosea 4:6)* They have not entered in because they do not understand the covenant and what God has made available to us.

To live under the commanded blessings of God you must know the blessings God has provided that are part of your inheritance as a child of God.

Living under the commanded blessings of God does not mean that you will never have any more financial problems, that you will never again face a physical battle or that you will never face any problems in your marriage or family relationships.

The children of Israel constantly faced battles, struggles and trials. But, as long as they kept their covenant with Almighty God, they were never defeated.

When you walk in covenant relationship with God and **know** it is His desire to pour His blessing upon you in every area of your life, you will be in a position to release your faith and take hold of whatever you need.

 God's blessing is the supernatural power that He imparts to His people through which He pours out His abundance into our lives.

Remember:

Everything that God has, he wants to pour into your life.

God released His blessing upon the children of Israel through those He had anointed and given this delegated authority. The blessing was released by speaking it aloud over the people. When they blessed the people, it was in God's Name and by His authority. No one could use the Name of God in blessing the people except those whom God had directed, whether as a prophet, priest or King. God spoke to Moses and gave him the words of blessing they were to speak over the people in His Name. The Father wanted His people to know and hear the words of this blessing spoken through Moses and Aaron as if He were speaking to them.

As we look at this Fatherly Priestly blessing, I pray God will open your eyes to see more clearly the blessings God wants to release in your life.

The Lord told Moses:

> *"Speak unto Aaron and unto his sons, saying, On this wise ye shall bless the children of Israel, saying unto them, The LORD bless thee, and keep thee: The LORD make his face shine upon thee, and be gracious unto thee: The LORD lift up his countenance upon thee, and give thee peace. And they shall put my name upon the children of Israel; and I will bless them."*
>
> *Numbers 6:23-27*

In essence, God was telling Moses, "I want you to speak this blessing over My people. I will place My Name upon them and I **will** bless them!"

As they spoke this blessing in His Name over the people, it released into their lives the awesome, supernatural power that is behind God's Name. This blessing, spoken in the power and authority of God's Name was not just a simple benediction or prayer. It released the supernatural power of God and His blessings upon them.

THE LORD BLESS THEE AND KEEP THEE."
(Numbers 6:24)

The very first thing the Father wanted His people to know and recognize was that he is the Divine Source of all blessing. It reveals His desire to lavish His blessings upon them as a father cherishes and desires to care for and give gifts to his children.

To walk under the commanded blessings of God, you must recognize God as your Divine Source of blessing. *"Every good and perfect gift is from above coming down from the Father of the heavenly lights, who does not change like shifting shadows."* (James 1:17, NIV)

Jesus said, *"If ye then, being evil, know how to give good gifts unto your children, how much more shall your Father which is in heaven give good things to them that ask him?"* (Matthew 7:11) He told His disciples, *"Do not be afraid, little flock, for your Father has chosen gladly to give you the kingdom."* (Luke 12:32, NAS)

Everything God has, He wants to

pour into your life.

As your Heavenly Father, God wants you to know He loves you with an everlasting love. He has chosen you and desires to release His richest blessing into your life.

In Numbers 6:24, we see our Heavenly Father has promised:

1. "I will bless you!"

2. "I will keep you!"

One of God's blessings upon His people today is that He has promised to protect, guard and keep us safe. We are under His watchful eye.

We are living in a day when it is no longer safe to walk down the street at night. Young children and our youth are no longer safe at school or in their own homes. Violence and death stalks the earth. But, God has pronounced His blessing upon His people and has said; "I will keep you! I will guard and protect you!" There is no greater security than to know that your are kept and protected by the power of Almighty God!

"THE LORD MAKE HIS FACE SHINE UPON THEE;"
(Numbers 6:25)

Throughout the Word, the face of God refers to His personality as either turned **toward** man or **away from** him. His face turned upon man in love and mercy is life and salvation. But, His face, turned against man, is destruction and death. *"For the eyes of the Lord are over the righteous, and his ears are open unto their prayers: but the face of the Lord is against them that do evil." (1 Peter 3:12)*

The blessing of the Father upon His people today is that His face will shine upon you. He will look upon you with great tenderness and love and His favor will be upon you. Just as a father looks for every opportunity to bestow his favor upon his children, our Heavenly Father watches over you to release His favor.

God's promised blessing upon your life is the greatest insurance policy we can ever have.

Just as the children of Israel enjoyed the blessing of God's favor, above all the other people upon the earth, God wants His people today to live under the blessing of His favor. David said, *"For surely, O LORD, you bless the righteous; you surround them with your favor as with a shield." (Psalm 5:12, NIV)*

God wants to bless you with His favor on the job, among your friends, in your neighborhood - wherever you go!

"...AND BE GRACIOUS UNTO THEE;"
(Numbers 6:25)

God has blessed us with His grace. Grace is the unmerited favor of God. We do not deserve God's blessings. We deserve His wrath. However, because of His grace and mercy, He spares us from all we deserve and blesses us.

"But God! So rich is He in His mercy! Because of and in order to satisfy the great and wonderful and intense love with which He loved us, Even when we were dead [slain] by [our own] shortcomings and trespasses, He made us alive together in fellowship and in union with Christ - He gave us the very life of Christ Himself, the same life with which He quickened Him. (For) it is by grace - by His favor and mercy which you did not deserve - that you are saved (delivered from judgment and made partakers of Christ's salvation.)

Ephesians 2:4-5, AMP

"THE LORD LIFT UP HIS COUNTENANCE UPON THEE AND GIVE THEE PEACE." (Numbers 6:26)

To "lift up" the countenance refers to pleasure and affection. Literally, this may be translated, "May Yahweh smile on you, and may he grant you well being." The Father's blessing upon our lives is that He turns His face toward us and looks upon us with an everlasting love. In other words, He smiles upon us. He takes great delight in us and desires to shower us with His affection.

Not only does He turn His fact toward us; He blesses us with peace. The word for peace in this verse is "Shalom." God blesses us with His "Shalom." The "Shalom" of God is much more than just the absence of war. Everything God has to offer is included; health, salvation, provision, spiritual riches, protection and all the blessings of God. It means **total well being** and to be universally blessed in every way!

"AND THEY SHALL PUT MY NAME UPON THE CHILDREN OF ISRAEL; AND I WILL BLESS THEM." (Numbers 6:27)

God gave Moses, Aaron and the priests the authority to use His Name in pronouncing blessing upon the people. This included all the blessings they could pronounce upon them to mark them as God's people.

Get ready!

God wants to mark you for His blessing!

As God's designated, spiritual authority spoke the blessing over the people; it linked them together with God's Name. All that is behind God's Name was supernaturally released into their lives.

In ancient times, names were very significant because they represented the individual. Names were very important to God. After He made a covenant with Abram, He changed Abram's name to "Abraham" which literally means "father of a multitude" (Genesis 17:5).

Jacob's name meant "the supplanter" which is "one who takes the place of and serves as a substitute." After his encounter with an angel, when he refused to let go until God blessed him, God changed his name to "Israel" which, in the Hebrew language, means, "ruling with God" (Genesis 32:28). Jesus changed Simon's name to Peter, which means, "stone or rock."

When Moses, Aaron and the priests lifted their hands toward the people and pronounced the Fatherly blessing upon them in God's Name, it meant:

1. God marked them as His own people.

2. God would bless them with all that is behind His Name. In other words, He would bless them with all that He has and is.

God put His Name on the line and said, "I will bless them!"

GOD DESIRES TO BLESS YOU
WITH ALL THAT HE HAS AND IS!

Today, we are marked by God's Name as His people and He has promised to bless us with all that he has and is!

To understand the full significance of the blessings God has pronounced upon you in His Name, it is important for you to know more about the power residing in God's Name.

God's Name represents all that is contained in His character: His love, mercy, forgiveness, provision, power, strength, grace and everything that He is. All that God is and all the power and authority He possesses is in His Name!

During His lifetime on earth, Jesus, in the form of human flesh, revealed God's Name to the world. He did not simply preach or teach about God's Name. He revealed it through His words and actions. He was a visible representation of all that God's Name means.

Jesus confronted Satan and all his evil principalities, defeated and stripped them of their power in His Father's Name. On the cross, when Jesus faced death, he did not one time think that God would forsake Him or that He would be defeated. He knew He would not fail.

How did He know? Jesus knew He could not fail because he was facing the power of the enemy in His Father's Name and that all the power and authority of heaven was behind that Name. Everything He said or did was in the power and authority of God's Name.

When Jesus ascended into Heaven, He transferred the power and authority of His Name to His Church!

God has placed His Name upon His people today and desires to bless you with all that His Name represents!

1. Jehovah-Jireh, the God who supplies.

This Name reveals God's ability and willingness to provide and supply all the needs of His people. When the children of Israel went through the wilderness, the blessings of Jehovah-Jireh were upon them! For forty years, He supernaturally supplied all their needs.

God has set His Name on you! You are a Joint-Heir with Jesus Christ. The unlimited, unsurpassing, incomparable blessings of God are at your disposal.

God Almighty is your Source and you have everything you need in His Name. Because the blessing of Jehovah-Jireh is upon you, whatever challenge or crisis you may go through God will be there with His provision. The Name of Jehovah-Jireh will open the doors of Heaven with His unlimited blessings and release them into your life.

 Because the blessing of Jehovah-Jireh is upon you, His provision will be released in whatever crisis you face.

2. El Shaddai - "The Almighty God."

Throughout the Word this Name reveals and emphasizes God's power to deliver His people out of the hands of their enemies. It reveals His all-sufficiency and Almighty power that is the supreme power over all. The word "shaddai" in Hebrew refers to a woman's breast. This expresses God's desire for His people to draw sustenance and strength from Him as a child is fed and nourished at its mother's breast.

With the blessing of El Shaddai upon you, you have nothing to fear because He will deliver you from the hands of your enemies. You will walk in His Almighty power as you draw what you need from Him.

3. Jehovah-Rapheka - the Lord our Healer.

God identified Himself to the children of Israel as their Healer. He said,

"...I am the Lord, (Jehovah-Rapheka) that healeth thee." He entered into a covenant with them and promised to remove sickness from among them as long as they walked in obedience to Him.

Jesus revealed and made known God's Name Jehovah-Repheka. He opened blind eyes, restored hearing, made the lame to walk and healed all that were oppressed of the devil. He revealed to the world that God is a healing God and that He has the power to destroy the works of the enemy and heal all those who trust in Him.

God has placed His Name upon you! Christ has given you power and authority in His Name. And, because the blessing of Jehovah-Rapheka is upon you, you can look sickness and disease in the eye and say, "I am conqueror over this disease because Jesus conquered it on the cross." I am blessed with healing in the Name of the Father. Healing is a blessing of My Father and because He has placed His Name upon me I can claim my healing!"

4. Jehovah Shalom - the Lord our peace.

As long as the children of Israel were walking in covenant relationship with God, His blessing of peace was upon them. In the world today there is no peace. Why? Because true and lasting peace is a by-product of a relationship with God. You cannot buy it. Peace is a fruit of the Spirit.

With the blessing of Jehovah Shalom upon your life, you can walk through the darkest hour of your life - the greatest time of sorrow and adversity and have His peace sustaining you.

With the blessing of His peace you cannot be defeated or compromised! Why? Because you are the blessed of God the Father with a peace that nothing can disturb.

Demons must run because you are blessed
of the Father with His supernatural blessing
and His Name is upon you!

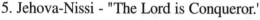

5. Jehova-Nissi - "The Lord is Conqueror.'

This Name reveals God as a mighty deliverer and conqueror that always conquers the enemies of His people. As long as the Israelites were obedient to Him, God (Jehovah-Nissi) conquered their enemies and made them victorious.

We are the people of God. With the blessing of Jehovah-Nissi upon us, we are the conquerors! When we pray in the power and authority of His Name, the gates of hell will not prevail against us!

We can walk up to the very gates of hell and say; "Release my daughter, my son, my mother," and immediately the demons will run because we are BLESSED OF THE FATHER WITH HIS SUPERNATURAL BLESSING AND HIS NAME IS UPON US!

It is time for the people of God to take hold of this blessing by faith and get spiritually violent on behalf of our families, and those bound by the powers of darkness all around us in our cities and neighborhoods. Jesus said, *"And from the days of John the Baptist until now the kingdom of heaven suffereth violence, and the violent take it by force."* *(Matthew 11:12)*

6. The Lord is My Shepherd.

David said, "The Lord is My Shepherd, I shall not want." With His blessing upon you, you will not want anything because He is with you to protect you and provide for you.

The blessing of the Lord will cause you to "lie down in green pastures" where your soul is made fat with His goodness. In the time of adversity, He will give you divine sufficiency for the hour.

7. Jehovah-Tiskenu - The Lord our Righteousness.

Our God is a holy God. God has said, "...*Be ye holy, for I am holy."* *(1 Peter 1:16)* We know that "...without holiness no man shall see the Lord." Our God who sits on His throne of holiness has blessed us with His righteousness.

There is nothing we can do to be made righteous. Our righteousness is as "filthy rags" before God. But, through Christ, we are cleansed and made holy and restored to a right standing with the Father.

Satan may try to intimidate you and make you think that you are unworthy of God's blessings. No one is worthy or deserving of His blessings, but because God loves us He has put His Name on us and blessed us with His righteousness!

We are cleansed and made holy by the blood of Jesus. And, because He has blessed us with His righteousness, we can come boldly to the Father in our time of need and receive His unmerited grace and mercy. We can come in the Name of Jesus and ask whatever we need and He will give it to us because we are the blessed of the Lord!

God has marked you and He has said, "I will bless you!" You are part of a Royal Seed - Jesus Christ and have inherited all the blessings of God. The royal blood flows in your veins. God has planned to pour out upon you His commanded blessings and to bless you with all that He has and is!

SPEAK THE BLESSINGS OF GOD OVER YOUR LIFE!

All of these blessings belong to you now! However, you must receive them by faith and act on his promises.

God has ordained that His blessing be passed from generation to generation through those He has anointed and given His authority. Moses, Aaron and the priests were the designated authority to speak His blessing over the people.

Fathers released the blessing of God over their households by speaking it over their wives and children. Abraham, Isaac and Jacob called their sons around them, laid hands upon them and blessed them in the Name of the Lord.

Eli, the Priest, spoke God's blessing over Hannah and God opened her womb and Samuel was born. After she had poured out her heart to God in prayer for a son, Eli blessed her. He said, "...Go in peace: and the God of Israel grant thee thy petition that thou hast asked of him." (1 Samuel 1:17) After years of barrenness, she conceived because the blessing of the Lord was upon her.

In the early Church, God raised up the fivefold ministry of apostles, prophets, evangelists, pastors and teachers as his delegated authority to minister to and bring the Church to full maturity.

The apostles were looked upon as spiritual fathers and were used by God to release and impart spiritual blessing to the Church. The

Apostle Paul laid his hands on his spiritual son, Timothy, and was used to impart gifts and blessings upon him. *"For this reason I remind you to fan into flame the gift of God, which is in you through the laying on of my hands." (2 Timothy 1:6, NIV)*

These apostolic fathers had the ability to impart blessings to their children in the faith. In his letter to the Church in Rome Paul said, *"For I long to see you, that I may impart unto you some spiritual gift, to the end ye may be established." (Romans 1:11)*

Paul closed his letter to the believers in Corinth by pronouncing God's blessing upon them. He said, *"The grace (favor and spiritual blessing) of the Lord Jesus Christ and the love of God and the presence and fellowship (the communion and sharing together, and participation) in the Holy Spirit be with you all." (2 Corinthians 13:14, AMP)*

By faith, speak the blessing of God upon your body, your marriage, your family, your finances – everything that belongs to you.

God is now raising up in the Church, true, apostolic spiritual fathers that He will use to strengthen and nurture the Church. A new generation of spiritual fathers is being enlisted by the Holy Spirit to provide the love, training, provision, reproduction and impartation He has ordained.

These apostolic spiritual fathers will be used by God to release and pronounce God's blessing upon spiritual sons and daughters.

Your Heavenly Father has marked you with His Name. He has released His blessings upon you. His blessings have been sealed with His oath. They cannot be reversed. He has said, "I will bless you!"

Receive the fullness of His blessings upon you, your family, your ministry and all that you have.

By faith, begin to speak the blessing of God upon your life, upon your physical body, upon your marriage, upon your children and upon your finances!

As a statement of your faith, say aloud:

"God has marked me with His Name. He is the Divine Source of all blessing. I am blessed of the Father with His supernatural blessing. He has blessed me with all that he has and is. By faith, I will walk under His commanded blessings!"

SCRIPTURE INDEX

GOD'S BLESSING IS HIS SUPERNATURAL POWER THAT HE IMPARTS TO HIS PEOPLE THROUGH WHICH HE POURS OUT HIS ABUNDANCE INTO OUR LIVES.

BLESS: The word "bless" in the Old Testament is translated from the Hebrew word "barak". It is used over 300 times in the Old Testament.

BLESSING: The word "blessing" is translated from the Hebrew word "berakah" which means "to bless...to release prosperity."

To have the blessing of God upon your life is to be blessed in every possible way.

OLD TESTAMENT PROMISES OF BLESSING:

GOD RELEASED BLESSING UPON ANIMALS

And God blessed them, saying, Be fruitful, and multiply, and fill the waters in the seas, and let fowl multiply in the earth. (Genesis 1:22)

GOD BLESSED ADAM AND EVE

And God blessed them, and God said unto them, Be fruitful, and multiply, and replenish the earth, and subdue it: and have dominion over the fish of the sea, and over the fowl of the air, and over every living thing that moveth upon the earth. (Genesis 1:28)

Male and female created he them; and blessed them, and called their name Adam, in the day when they were created. (Genesis 5:2)

GOD PRONOUNCED BLESSING UPON THE SABBATH
And God blessed the seventh day, and sanctified it: because that in it he had rested from all his work which God created and made. (Genesis 2:3)

GOD RELEASED HIS BLESSING UPON NOAH AND HIS SONS
And God blessed Noah and his sons, and said unto them, Be fruitful, and multiply, and replenish the earth. (Genesis 9:1)

GOD'S BLESSING PRONOUNCED UPON ABRAHAM
And I will make of thee a great nation, and I will bless thee, and make thy name great; and thou shalt be a blessing: And I will bless them that bless thee, and curse him that curseth thee: and in thee shall all families of the earth be blessed. (Genesis 12:2-3)

That in blessing I will bless thee, and in multiplying I will multiply thy seed as the stars of the heaven, and as the sand which is upon the sea shore; and thy seed shall possess the gate of his enemies; And in thy seed shall all the nations of the earth be blessed; because thou hast obeyed my voice. (Genesis 22:17-18)

And Abraham was old, and well stricken in age: and the LORD had blessed Abraham in all things. (Genesis 24:1)

And the LORD hath blessed my master greatly; and he is become great: and he hath given him flocks, and herds, and silver, and gold, and menservants, and maidservants, and camels, and asses. (Genesis 24:35)

GOD'S BLESSING PRONOUNCED UPON ISAAC
And it came to pass after the death of Abraham, that God blessed his son Isaac; and Isaac dwelt by the well Lahai-roi. (Genesis 25:11)

Sojourn in this land, and I will be with thee, and will bless thee; for unto thee, and unto thy seed, I will give all these countries, and I will perform the oath which I sware unto Abraham thy father; (Genesis 26:3)

And the LORD appeared unto him the same night, and said, I am the God of Abraham thy father: fear not, for I am with thee, and will bless thee, and multiply thy seed for my servant Abraham's sake. (Genesis 26:24)

Then Isaac sowed in that land, and received in the same year an hundredfold: and the LORD blessed him. And the man waxed great, and went forward, and grew until he became very great: F o r he had possession of flocks, and possession of herds, and great store of servants: and the Philistines envied him. (Genesis 26:12-14)

KING ABIMILECH RECOGNIZED GOD'S BLESSING UPON ISAAC

That thou wilt do us no hurt, as we have not touched thee, and as we have done unto thee nothing but good, and have sent thee away in peace: thou art now the blessed of the LORD. (Genesis 26:29)

REBEKAH'S FAMILY SPOKE A BLESSING UPON HER

And they blessed Rebekah, and said unto her, Thou art our sister, be thou the mother of thousands of millions, and let thy seed possess the gate of those which hate them. (Genesis 24:60)

GOD'S BLESSING UPON ISHMAEL

And as for Ishmael, I have heard thee: Behold, I have blessed him, and will make him fruitful, and will multiply him exceedingly; twelve princes shall he beget, and I will make him a great nation. (Genesis 17:20)

ISAAC PRONOUNCED GOD'S BLESSING UPON JACOB

And God Almighty bless thee, and make thee fruitful, and multiply thee, that thou mayest be a multitude of people; And give thee the blessing of Abraham, to thee, and to thy seed with thee; that thou mayest inherit the land wherein thou art a stranger, which God gave unto Abraham. (Genesis 28:2-4)

And, behold, the LORD stood above it, and said, I am the LORD God of Abraham thy father, and the God of Isaac: the land whereon

73

thou liest, to thee will I give it, and to thy seed; And thy seed shall be as the dust of the earth, and thou shalt spread abroad to the west, and to the east, and to the north, and to the south: and in thee and in thy seed shall all the families of the earth be blessed. And, behold, I am with thee, and will keep thee in all places whither thou goest, and will bring thee again into this land; for I will not leave thee, until I have done that which I have spoken to thee of. (Genesis 28:13-15)

JACOB WRESTLED WITH THE ANGEL OF THE LORD FOR GOD'S BLESSING

And he said, Let me go, for the day breaketh. And he said, I will not let thee go, except thou bless me. And he said unto him, What is thy name? And he said, Jacob. And he said, Thy name shall be called no more Jacob, but Israel: for as a prince hast thou power with God and with men, and hast prevailed. And Jacob asked him, and said, Tell me, I pray thee, thy name. And he said, Wherefore is it that thou dost ask after my name? And he blessed him there. (Genesis 32: 26-29)

GOD PRONOUNCED BLESSING AND CHANGED JACOB'S NAME

And God appeared unto Jacob again, when he came out of Padan-aram, and blessed him. And God said unto him, Thy name is Jacob: thy name shall not be called any more Jacob, but Israel shall be thy name: and he called his name Israel. And God said unto him, I am God Almighty: be fruitful and multiply; a nation and a company of nations shall be of thee, and kings shall come out of thy loins; And the land which I gave Abraham and Isaac, to thee I will give it, and to thy seed after thee will I give the land. (Genesis 35:9-12)

JACOB PRONOUNCED GOD'S BLESSING UPON JOSEPH AND HIS TWO SONS

And Joseph said unto his father, They are my sons, whom God hath given me in this place. And he said, Bring them, I pray thee, unto me, and I will bless them. (Genesis 48:9)

And Joseph brought them out from between his knees, and he bowed himself with his face to the earth. And Joseph took them both, Ephraim in his right hand toward Israel's left hand, and Manasseh in his left hand toward Israel's right hand, and brought them near unto him. And Israel stretched out his right hand, and laid it upon Ephraim's head, who was the younger, and his left hand upon Manasseh's head, guiding his hands wittingly; for Manasseh was the firstborn. And he blessed Joseph, and said, God, before whom my fathers Abraham and Isaac did walk, the God which fed me all my life long unto this day, The Angel which redeemed me from all evil, bless the lads; and let my name be named on them, and the name of my fathers Abraham and Isaac; and let them grow into a multitude in the midst of the earth. (Genesis 48:12-16)

And he blessed them that day, saying, In thee shall Israel bless, saying, God make thee as Ephraim and as Manasseh: and he set Ephraim before Manasseh. (Genesis 48:20)

JACOB'S SPECIAL BLESSING UPON JOSEPH

Even by the God of thy father, who shall help thee; and by the Almighty, who shall bless thee with blessings of heaven above, blessings of the deep that lieth under, blessings of the breasts, and of the womb: The blessings of thy father have prevailed above the blessings of my progenitors unto the utmost bound of the everlasting hills: they shall be on the head of Joseph, and on the crown of the head of him that was separate from his brethren. (Genesis 49:25-26)

GOD'S BLESSING UPON POTIPHAR FOR JOSEPH'S SAKE

And it came to pass from the time that he had made him overseer in his house, and over all that he had, that the LORD blessed the Egyptian's house for Joseph's sake; and the blessing of the LORD was upon all that he had in the house, and in the field. (Genesis 39:5)

GOD'S PROMISE TO BLESS MOSES

An altar of earth thou shalt make unto me, and shalt sacrifice thereon thy burnt offerings, and thy peace offerings, thy sheep, and thine oxen: in all places where I record my name I will come unto thee, and I will bless thee. (Exodus 20:24)

GOD'S PROMISED BLESSING OF HEALTH

And ye shall serve the LORD your God, and he shall bless thy bread, and thy water; and I will take sickness away from the midst of thee. (Exodus 23:25)

GOD'S INSTRUCTION FOR AARON AND HIS SONS TO PRONOUNCE HIS BLESSING UPON ISRAEL

Speak unto Aaron and unto his sons, saying, On this wise ye shall bless the children of Israel, saying unto them, The LORD bless thee, and keep thee: The LORD make his face shine upon thee, and be gracious unto thee: The LORD lift up his countenance upon thee, and give thee peace. And they shall put my name upon the children of Israel; and I will bless them. (Numbers 6:23-27)

MOSES PRONOUNCED BLESSING UPON THE PEOPLE

And Moses did look upon all the work, and, behold, they had done it as the LORD had commanded, even so had they done it: and Moses blessed them. (Exodus 39:43)

And Aaron lifted up his hand toward the people, and blessed them, and came down from offering of the sin offering, and the burnt offering, and peace offerings. And Moses and Aaron went into the tabernacle of the congregation, and came out, and blessed the people: and the glory of the LORD appeared unto all the people. And there came a fire out from before the LORD, and consumed upon the altar the burnt offering and the fat: which when all the people saw, they shouted, and fell on their faces. (Leviticus 9:22-24)

GOD'S BLESSING CANNOT BE REVERSED

And God said unto Balaam, Thou shalt not go with them; thou shalt not curse the people: for they are blessed. (Numbers 22:12)

Behold, I have received commandment to bless: and he hath blessed; and I cannot reverse it. (Numbers 23:20)

GOD TURNED CURSE INTO BLESSING

Nevertheless the LORD thy God would not hearken unto Balaam; but the LORD thy God turned the curse into a blessing unto thee, because the LORD thy God loved thee. (Deuteronomy 23:5)

GOD'S PROMISED BLESSINGS FOR OBEDIENCE

Behold, I set before you this day a blessing and a curse; A blessing, if ye obey the commandments of the LORD your God, which I command you this day:

(Deuteronomy 11:26-27)

And he will love thee, and bless thee, and multiply thee: he will also bless the fruit of thy womb, and the fruit of thy land, thy corn, and thy wine, and thine oil, the increase of thy kine, and the flocks of thy sheep, in the land which he sware unto thy fathers to give thee. (Deuteronomy 7:13)

Save when there shall be no poor among you; for the LORD shall greatly bless thee in the land which the LORD thy God giveth thee for an inheritance to possess it: Only if thou carefully hearken unto the voice of the LORD thy God, to observe to do all these commandments which I command thee this day. For the LORD thy God blesseth thee, as he promised thee: and thou shalt lend unto many nations, but thou shalt not borrow; and thou shalt reign over many nations, but they shall not reign over thee. (Deuteronomy 15:4-6)

LEVITES CHOSEN TO BLESS ISRAEL IN GOD'S NAME

At that time the LORD separated the tribe of Levi, to bear the ark of the covenant of the LORD, to stand before the LORD to minister unto him, and to bless in his name, unto this day. (Deuteronomy 10:8)

And the priests the sons of Levi shall come near; for them the LORD thy God hath chosen to minister unto him, and to bless in the name of the LORD; and by their word shall every controversy and every stroke be tried: (Deuteronomy 21:5)

The sons of Amram; Aaron and Moses: and Aaron was separated, that he should sanctify the most holy things, he and his sons for ever, to burn incense before the LORD, to minister unto him, and to bless in his name for ever. (1 Chronicles 23:13)

GOD'S JUBILEE BLESSING

Then I will command my blessing upon you in the sixth year, and it shall bring forth fruit for three years. (Leviticus 25:21)

GOD'S BLESSING FOR MINISTERING TO THE POOR

Thou shalt surely give him, and thine heart shall not be grieved when thou givest unto him: because that for this thing the LORD thy God shall bless thee in all thy works, and in all that thou puttest thine hand unto. (Deuteronomy 15:10)

Seven days shalt thou keep a solemn feast unto the LORD thy God in the place which the LORD shall choose: because the LORD thy God shall bless thee in all thine increase, and in all the works of thine hands, therefore thou shalt surely rejoice. (Deuteronomy 16:15)

PROMISE OF GOD'S COMMANDED BLESSINGS

The LORD shall command the blessing upon thee in thy storehouses, and in all that thou settest thine hand unto; and he shall bless thee in the land which the LORD thy God giveth thee. (Deuteronomy 28:8)

The LORD shall open unto thee his good treasure, the heaven to give the rain unto thy land in his season, and to bless all the work of thine hand: and thou shalt lend unto many nations, and thou shalt not borrow. (Deuteronomy 28:12)

In that I command thee this day to love the LORD thy God, to walk in his ways, and to keep his commandments and his statutes and his judgments, that thou mayest live and multiply: and the LORD thy God shall bless thee in the land whither thou goest to possess it. (Deuteronomy 30:16)

GOD'S BLESSING PRONOUNCED UPON ISRAEL ACCORDING TO GOD'S DIRECTION

And all Israel, and their elders, and officers, and their judges, stood on this side the ark and on that side before the priests the Levites, which bare the ark of the covenant of the LORD, as well the stranger, as he that was born among them; half of them over against mount Gerizim, and half of them over against mount Ebal; as Moses the servant of the LORD had commanded before, that they should bless the people of Israel. (Joshua 8:33)

GOD'S BLESSING IN THE WILDERNESS

For the LORD thy God hath blessed thee in all the works of thy hand: he knoweth thy walking through this great wilderness: these forty years the LORD thy God hath been with thee; thou hast lacked nothing. (Deuteronomy 2:7)

BLESSED ABOVE ALL PEOPLE

Thou shalt be blessed above all people: there shall not be male or female barren among you, or among your cattle. (Deuteronomy 7:14)

REJOICE IN GOD'S BLESSINGS

And there ye shall eat before the LORD your God, and ye shall rejoice in all that ye put your hand unto, ye and your households, wherein the LORD thy God hath blessed thee. (Deuteronomy 12:7)

BLESSINGS WHEREVER YOU GO

Blessed shalt thou be in the city, and blessed shalt thou be in the field. (Deuteronomy 28:3)

BLESSINGS UPON CHILDREN AND ALL THAT YOU HAVE

Blessed shall be the fruit of thy body, and the fruit of thy ground, and the fruit of thy cattle, the increase of thy kine, and the flocks of thy sheep. (Deuteronomy 28:4)

BLESSINGS UPON YOUR PROVISION

Blessed shall be thy basket and thy store. (Deuteronomy 28:5)

GOD'S BLESSING WILL REST UPON YOU WHEREVER YOU GO!

Blessed shalt thou be when thou comest in, and blessed shalt thou be when thou goest out. (Deuteronomy 28:6)

The LORD shall cause thine enemies that rise up against thee to be smitten before thy face: they shall come out against thee one way, and flee before thee seven ways. (Deuteronomy 28:7)

And the LORD shall make thee plenteous in goods, in the fruit of thy body, and in the fruit of thy cattle, and in the fruit of thy ground, in the land which the LORD sware unto thy fathers to give thee. The LORD shall open unto thee his good treasure, the heaven to give the rain unto thy land in his season, and to bless all the work of thine hand: and thou shalt lend unto many nations, and thou shalt not borrow. And the LORD shall make thee the head, and not the tail; and thou shalt be above only, and thou shalt not be beneath; if that thou hearken unto the commandments of the LORD thy God, which I command thee this day, to observe and to do them: (Deuteronomy 28:11-13)

JOSHUA RELEASED BLESSINGS UPON THE CHILDREN OF ISRAEL

And Joshua blessed him, and gave unto Caleb the son of Jephunneh Hebron for an inheritance. (Joshua 14:13)

And the children of Joseph spake unto Joshua, saying, Why hast thou given me but one lot and one portion to inherit, seeing I am a great people, forasmuch as the LORD hath blessed me hitherto? (Joshua 17:14)

So Joshua blessed them, and sent them away: and they went unto their tents. Now to the one half of the tribe of Manasseh Moses had given possession in Bashan: but unto the other half thereof gave Joshua among their brethren on this side Jordan westward. And when Joshua sent them away also unto their tents, then he blessed them, (Joshua 22:6-7)

OBEDEDOM BLESSED BECAUSE OF ARK OF COVENANT

And the ark of the LORD continued in the house of Obededom the Gittite three months: and the LORD blessed Obededom, and all his household. And it was told king David, saying, The LORD hath blessed the house of Obededom, and all that pertaineth unto him, because of the ark of God. So David went and brought up the ark of God from the house of Obededom into the city of David with gladness. (2 Samuel 6:11-12)

DAVID RELEASED BLESSING UPON THE PEOPLE

And as soon as David had made an end of offering burnt offerings and peace offerings, he blessed the people in the name of the LORD of hosts. (2 Samuel 6:18)

And when David had made an end of offering the burnt offerings and the peace offerings, he blessed the people in the name of the LORD. (2 Chronicles 16:2)

81

DAVID RELEASED BLESSING UPON ABSALOM

And the king said to Absalom, Nay, my son, let us not all now go, lest we be chargeable unto thee. And he pressed him: howbeit he would not go, but blessed him. (2 Samuel 13:25)

DAVID'S PRAYER FOR GOD'S PROMISED BLESSING

Therefore now let it please thee to bless the house of thy servant, that it may continue for ever before thee: for thou, O Lord GOD, hast spoken it: and with thy blessing let the house of thy servant be blessed for ever. (2 Samuel 7:29)

JABEZ'S PRAYER FOR GOD'S BLESSING

And Jabez called on the God of Israel, saying, Oh that thou wouldest bless me indeed, and enlarge my coast, and that thine hand might be with me, and that thou wouldest keep me from evil, that it may not grieve me! And God granted him that which he requested. (2 Chronicles 4:10)

GOD'S BLESSING RESTED UPON SOLOMON

And the king turned his face about, and blessed all the congregation of Israel: (and all the congregation of Israel stood;) And he said, Blessed be the LORD God of Israel, which spake with his mouth unto David my father, and hath with his hand fulfilled it, saying, (1 Kings 8:14-15)

And he stood, and blessed all the congregation of Israel with a loud voice, saying, Blessed be the LORD, that hath given rest unto his people Israel, according to all that he promised: there hath not failed one word of all his good promise, which he promised by the hand of Moses his servant. (1 Kings 8:55-56)

PRIESTS AND LEVITES BLESS THE PEOPLE

Then the priests the Levites arose and blessed the people: and their voice was heard, and their prayer came up to his holy dwelling place, even unto heaven. (2 Chronicles 30:27)

GOD'S BLESSINGS POURED OUT IN ABUNDANCE

And Azariah the chief priest of the house of Zadok answered him, and said, Since the people began to bring the offerings into the house of the LORD, we have had enough to eat, and have left plenty: for the LORD hath blessed his people; and that which is left is this great store. (2 Chronicles 31:10)

GOD'S BLESSINGS RESTED UPON JOB

Hast not thou made an hedge about him, and about his house, and about all that he hath on every side? thou hast blessed the work of his hands, and his substance is increased in the land. (Job 1:10)

So the LORD blessed the latter end of Job more than his beginning: for he had fourteen thousand sheep, and six thousand camels, and a thousand yoke of oxen, and a thousand she asses. (Job 42:12)

GOD'S PROMISE TO RAIN DOWN SHOWERS OF BLESSINGS

And I will make them and the places round about my hill a blessing; and I will cause the shower to come down in his season; there shall be showers of blessing. (Ezekiel 34:26)

GOD'S PROPHETIC PROMISE TO MAKE ISRAEL A BLESSING

And it shall come to pass, that as ye were a curse among the heathen, O house of Judah, and house of Israel; so will I save you, and ye shall be a blessing: fear not, but let your hands be strong. (Zechariah 8:13)

GOD'S BLESSING UPON THOSE WHO TITHE

Bring ye all the tithes into the storehouse, that there may be meat in mine house, and prove me now herewith, saith the LORD of hosts, if I will not open you the windows of heaven, and pour you out a blessing, that there shall not be room enough to receive it. (Malachi 3:10)

GIVING ACCORDING TO GOD'S BLESSING

Every man shall give as he is able, according to the blessing of the LORD thy God which he hath given thee. (Deuteronomy 16:17)

GOD'S BLESSING OF PROSPERITY UPON THE GODLY

Blessed is the man that walketh not in the counsel of the ungodly, nor standeth in the way of sinners, nor sitteth in the seat of the scornful. But his delight is in the law of the LORD; and in his law doth he meditate day and night. And he shall be like a tree planted by the rivers of water, that bringeth forth his fruit in his season; his leaf also shall not wither; and whatsoever he doeth shall prosper. (Psalms 1:1-3)

GOD'S BLESSING UPON THOSE WHO TRUST HIM

Kiss the Son, lest he be angry, and ye perish from the way, when his wrath is kindled but a little. Blessed are all they that put their trust in him. (Psalms 2-12)

O taste and see that the LORD is good: blessed is the man that trusteth in him. (Psalms 34:8)

Blessed is that man that maketh the LORD his trust, and respecteth not the proud, nor such as turn aside to lies. (Psalms 40:4)

O LORD of hosts, blessed is the man that trusteth in thee. (Psalms 84:12)

Blessed is the man that trusteth in the LORD, and whose hope the LORD is. (Jeremiah 17:7)

GOD'S BLESSINGS BELONG TO PURE IN HEART

Who shall ascend into the hill of the LORD? or who shall stand in his holy place? He that hath clean hands, and a pure heart; who hath not lifted up his soul unto vanity, nor sworn deceitfully.
He shall receive the blessing from the LORD, and righteousness from the God of his salvation. (Psalms 24:3-5)

GOD'S PROMISED BLESSING OF FAVOR
For thou, LORD, wilt bless the righteous; with favour wilt thou compass him as with a shield. (Psalms 5:12)

GOD'S PROMISED BLESSING OF STRENGTH AND PEACE
The LORD will give strength unto his people; the LORD will bless his people with peace. (Psalms 29:11)

GOD'S BLESSING OF FORGIVENESS
Blessed is he whose transgression is forgiven, whose sin is covered.

Blessed is the man unto whom the LORD imputeth not iniquity, and in whose spirit there is no guile. (Psalms 32:1-2)

GOD'S BLESSING IS UPON HIS SEED
I have been young, and now am old; yet have I not seen the righteous forsaken, nor his seed begging bread. He is ever merciful, and lendeth; and his seed is blessed. (Psalms 37:25-26)

GOD'S BLESSING UPON THOSE WHO HELP THE POOR
Blessed is he that considereth the poor: the LORD will deliver him in time of trouble. The LORD will preserve him, and keep him alive; and he shall be blessed upon the earth: and thou wilt not deliver him unto the will of his enemies. The LORD will strengthen him upon the bed of languishing: thou wilt make all his bed in his sickness. (Psalms 41:1-3)

He that hath a bountiful eye shall be blessed; for he giveth of his bread to the poor. (Proverbs 22:9)

GOD'S PEOPLE BLESSED AND WALK IN HIS GLORY
Blessed is the people that know the joyful sound: they shall walk, O LORD, in the light of thy countenance. In thy name shall they rejoice all the day: and in thy righteousness shall they be exalted.

For thou art the glory of their strength: and in thy favour our horn shall be exalted. (Psalms 89:15)

GOD'S BLESSING IS UPON THOSE HE CHASTENS
Blessed is the man whom thou chastenest, O LORD, and teachest him out of thy law; That thou mayest give him rest from the days of adversity, until the pit be digged for the wicked. For the LORD will not cast off his people, neither will he forsake his inheritance. (Psalms 94:12-14)

GOD'S BLESSING IS UPON THE RIGHTEOUS
Blessed are they that keep judgment, and he that doeth righteousness at all times. (Psalms 196:3)

Blessed are the undefiled in the way, who walk in the law of the LORD. Blessed are they that keep his testimonies, and that seek him with the whole heart. They also do no iniquity: they walk in his ways. (Psalms 119:1-3)

Now therefore hearken unto me, O ye children: for blessed are they that keep my ways. (Proverbs 8:32)

GOD'S BLESSING OF INCREASE UPON HIS PEOPLE
The LORD hath been mindful of us: he will bless us; he will bless the house of Israel; he will bless the house of Aaron. He will bless them that fear the LORD, both small and great. The LORD shall increase you more and more, you and your children. Ye are blessed of the LORD which made heaven and earth. The heaven, even the heavens, are the LORD's: but the earth hath he given to the children of men. (Psalms 115:12-16)

GOD'S BLESSING IS UPON THOSE WHO FEAR HIM
Praise ye the LORD. Blessed is the man that feareth the LORD, that delighteth greatly in his commandments. His seed shall be mighty upon earth: the generation of the upright shall be blessed. (Psalms 112:1-2)

He will bless them that fear the LORD, both small and great. (Psalms 115:13)

Blessed is every one that feareth the LORD; that walketh in his ways. (Psalms 128:1)

Behold, that thus shall the man be blessed that feareth the LORD. (Psalms 128:4)

GOD'S BLESSING UPON THOSE WHO WAIT UPON HIM

Blessed is the man that heareth me, watching daily at my gates, waiting at the posts of my doors. (Proverbs 8:34)

And therefore will the LORD wait, that he may be gracious unto you, and therefore will he be exalted, that he may have mercy upon you: for the LORD is a God of judgment: blessed are all they that wait for him. (Isaiah 30:18)

GOD'S BLESSING IS UPON THE SEED OF THE RIGHTEOUS

The just man walketh in his integrity: his children are blessed after him. (Proverbs 20:7)

GOD'S BLESSING RELEASED THROUGH PRAISE

Let the people praise thee, O God; let all the people praise thee. Then shall the earth yield her increase; and God, even our own God, shall bless us. God shall bless us; and all the ends of the earth shall fear him. (Psalms 67:5-7)

GOD'S BLESSING UPON THOSE WHO KEEP THE SABBATH HOLY

Blessed is the man that doeth this, and the son of man that layeth hold on it; that keepeth the sabbath from polluting it, and keepeth his hand from doing any evil. (Isaiah 56:2)

SEED OF THE RIGHTEOUS BLESSED

And their seed shall be known among the Gentiles, and their offspring among the people: all that see them shall acknowledge them, that they are the seed which the LORD hath blessed. (Isaiah 61:9)

They shall not labour in vain, nor bring forth for trouble; for they are the seed of the blessed of the LORD, and their offspring with them. (Isaiah 65:23)

NEW TESTAMENT BLESSINGS

IN HIS FIRST SERMON, JESUS RELEASED BLESSING

Blessed are the poor in spirit: for theirs is the kingdom of heaven. (Matthew 5:3)

Blessed are they that mourn: for they shall be comforted. (Matthew 5:4)

Blessed are the meek: for they shall inherit the earth. (Matthew 5:5)

Blessed are they which do hunger and thirst after righteousness: for they shall be filled. (Matthew 5:6)

Blessed are the merciful: for they shall obtain mercy. (Matthew 5:7)

Blessed are the pure in heart: for they shall see God. (Matthew 5:8)

Blessed are the peacemakers: for they shall be called the children of God. (Matthew 5:9)

Blessed are they which are persecuted for righteousness' sake: for theirs is the kingdom of heaven. (Matthew 5:10)

Blessed are ye, when men shall revile you, and persecute you, and shall say all manner of evil against you falsely, for my sake. (Matthew 5:11)

JESUS BLESSED AND MULTIPLIED FOOD TO FEED MULTITUDE

And he commanded the multitude to sit down on the grass, and took the five loaves, and the two fishes, and looking up to heaven, he blessed, and brake, and gave the loaves to his disciples, and the disciples to the multitude. (Matthew 14:19)

JESUS PRONOUNCED BLESSING UPON PETER

And Jesus answered and said unto him, Blessed art thou, Simon Barjona: for flesh and blood hath not revealed it unto thee, but my Father which is in heaven. (Matthew 16:17)

BLESSING PRONOUNCED UPON THOSE WHO ARE DOING HIS WILL WHEN HE RETURNS

Blessed is that servant, whom his lord when he cometh shall find so doing. (Matthew 24:46)

Then shall the King say unto them on his right hand, Come, ye blessed of my Father, inherit the kingdom prepared for you from the foundation of the world: (Matthew 25:34)

JESUS SPEAKS BLESSING UPON THOSE WHO HEAR AND OBEY GOD'S WORD

But he said, Yea rather, blessed are they that hear the word of God, and keep it. (Luke 11:28)

BLESSING PRONOUNCED UPON THOSE WHO WATCH FOR CHRIST'S COMING

Blessed are those servants, whom the lord when he cometh shall find watching: verily I say unto you, that he shall gird himself, and make them to sit down to meat, and will come forth and serve them. And if he shall come in the second watch, or come in the third watch, and find them so, blessed are those servants. (Luke 12:37-38)

JESUS RELEASED HIS BLESSING BEFORE HE ASCENDED INTO HEAVEN

And he led them out as far as to Bethany, and he lifted up his hands, and blessed them. And it came to pass, while he blessed them, he was parted from them, and carried up into heaven. (Luke 24:50-51)

JESUS RELEASED BLESSING UPON THOSE WHO BELIEVE IN HIM

Jesus saith unto him, Thomas, because thou hast seen me, thou hast believed: blessed are they that have not seen, and yet have believed. (John 20:29)

BLESSING RELEASED UPON THOSE WHO GIVE
I have shewed you all things, how that so labouring ye ought to support the weak, and to remember the words of the Lord Jesus, how he said, It is more blessed to give than to receive. (Acts 20:35)

BLESSING OF ABRAHAM RELEASED TO US THROUGH CHRIST
That the blessing of Abraham might come on the Gentiles through Jesus Christ; that we might receive the promise of the Spirit through faith. (Galatians 3:14)

ESAU FAILS TO TAKE POSSESSION OF HIS BLESSING
For ye know how that afterward, when he would have inherited the blessing, he was rejected: for he found no place of repentance, though he sought it carefully with tears. (Hebrews 12:17)

JESUS' COMMAND TO BLESS
But I say unto you, Love your enemies, bless them that curse you, do good to them that hate you, and pray for them which despitefully use you, and persecute you; (Matthew 5:44)

Bless them that curse you, and pray for them which despitefully use you. (Luke 6:28)

Bless them which persecute you: bless, and curse not. (Romans 12:14)

WE ARE CALLED TO RELEASE BLESSING
Not rendering evil for evil, or railing for railing: but contrariwise blessing; knowing that ye are thereunto called, that ye should inherit a blessing. (1 Peter 3:9)

JESUS SENT TO BLESS US WITH SALVATION
Unto you first God, having raised up his Son Jesus, sent him to bless you, in turning away every one of you from his iniquities. (Acts 3:26)

WE INHERIT GOD'S BLESSING THROUGH FAITH
And the scripture, foreseeing that God would justify the heathen through faith, preached before the gospel unto Abraham, saying, In thee

shall all nations be blessed. So then they which be of faith are blessed with faithful Abraham. (Galatians 3:8-9)

WE ARE BLESSED WITH ALL SPIRITUAL BLESSINGS
Blessed be the God and Father of our Lord Jesus Christ, who hath blessed us with all spiritual blessings in heavenly places in Christ: (Ephesians 1:3)

MELCHISEDEC BLESSED ABRAHAM
For this Melchisedec, king of Salem, priest of the most high God, who met Abraham returning from the slaughter of the kings, and blessed him; (Hebrews 7:1)

But he whose descent is not counted from them received tithes of Abraham, and blessed him that had the promises. (Hebrews 7:6)

BLESSINGS RELEASED BY FAITH
By faith Isaac blessed Jacob and Esau concerning things to come. By faith Jacob, when he was a dying, blessed both the sons of Joseph; and worshipped, leaning upon the top of his staff. (Hebrews 11:20-21)

BLESSING PRONOUNCED UPON THOSE WHO ENDURE TEMPTATION
Blessed is the man that endureth temptation: for when he is tried, he shall receive the crown of life, which the Lord hath promised to them that love him. (James 1:12)

BLESSING PRONOUNCED UPON THOSE WHO DO THE WORK OF GOD
But whoso looketh into the perfect law of liberty, and continueth therein, he being not a forgetful hearer, but a doer of the work, this man shall be blessed in his deed. (James 1:25)

SEVEN BLESSINGS IN REVELATION
Blessed is he that readeth, and they that hear the words of this prophecy, and keep those things which are written therein: for the time is at hand. (Revelation 1:3)

And I heard a voice from heaven saying unto me, Write, **Blessed** are the dead which die in the Lord from henceforth: Yea, saith the Spirit, that they may rest from their labours; and their works do follow them. (Revelation 14:13)

Behold, I come as a thief. **Blessed** is he that watcheth, and keepeth his garments, lest he walk naked, and they see his shame. (Revelation 16:15)

And he saith unto me, Write, **Blessed** are they which are called unto the marriage supper of the Lamb. And he saith unto me, These are the true sayings of God. (Revelation 19:9)

Blessed and holy is he that hath part in the first resurrection: on such the second death hath no power, but they shall be priests of God and of Christ, and shall reign with him a thousand years. (Revelation 20:6)

Behold, I come quickly: **blessed** is he that keepeth the sayings of the prophecy of this book. (Revelation 22:7)

Blessed are they that do his commandments, that they may have right to the tree of life, and may enter in through the gates into the city. (Revelation 22:14)